LITTLE

BIG

MEN

The Road to Williamsport

Gary Yeagle

Gary M Yeagle

Publisher: Goose Creek Publishers, Inc.
4227 Vermont Avenue
Louisville, KY 40211
502-384-5109 Ph./Fax
goosecreekpublishers.com

ISBN: Trade Casebound 1-59633-006-6 $24.95

Printed in the USA
All Right Reserved

10 9 8 7 6 5 4 3 2

Available in retail stores.

TABLE OF CONTENTS

Dedication

In Memory of Brian Davis
Our Angel in the Outfileld

Acknowledgements

I have many individuals and organizations to thank for their cooperation and valuable insight in writing this book. First of all, I'd like to express many thanks to two of my childhood friends who not only grew up with me in Williamsport, but who played the game of Little League Baseball with me. Philip Lesko, still a resident of Williamsport and pastor of Trinity Gospel Church was the 1959 batting champion at the Original Field and Jim Collins, a resident and local businessman, was the 1958 batting champ, also at the Original Field.

Heartfelt thanks to my two close friends who helped me to recall many childhood moments of not only growing up in Williamsport, but learning and playing the game of Little League Baseball.

I am also deeply indebted to Bill Byham, a former public school teacher who lives in Williamsport. To say that Bill is involved in Little League is without a doubt an accurate statement. Walking from his front door just down a slight hill is where the Little League Complex is situated. Bill has announced Little League World Series games for forty-two years. Between 1946-52 Bill pitched in the Minor Leagues for both the Giants and St. Louis organizations. He currently writes two columns in Williamsport and was kind enough to take the time to compose the foreward for this book. Thanks Bill, not only for your words of wisdom but also for the valuable information you gave me as we sat around my mother's kitchen table when I first decided to write this story.

I am grateful to Joe Girio who took the time to sit down with me at his office in Williamsport and share his delightful experience of being a "team uncle" for the 2002 Kentucky team. As one of two individuals assigned to the Valley Sports team, Joe took responsibility for their needs and comfort during their stay at the Little League Complex from the time they stepped off the plane until they prepared for the return trip home. Thanks not only to Joe, but to the numerous team hosts and volunteers who give of their time to make sure the teams who journey to Williamsport will indeed have the time of their lives.

I wish to thank two different newspapers who did a unique job of daily coverage during the Little League World Series. The Williamsport Sun Gazette's daily articles of games played and mixed topics of interest greatly assisted me in putting together information for the book. The Courier-Journal in Louisville made available over eighty articles of interest in regard to Valley Sports' incredible journey toward the title of World Champions and finally their return home to Louisville. Many thanks to Mike Flanders and his staff at Shively Sporting Goods in Louisville for facts on the promotion and sale of Valley Sports tee shirts. Eric Titius and his employees at BW3's, also in Louisville, were extremely helpful for supplying highlights of local fan interest at their sports establishments.

I will never forget the wonderful group of individuals who are employed at Little League in Williamsport. The cooperation that I received from this organization was nothing less than awesome. Steve Keener, president and CEO of Little League, was kind enough to invite me into his office and listen to my idea for this book. Lance Van Auken, Senior Communications Executive, after asking me what I needed, offered me complete access to the Little League Complex. What a thrill it was for me to go out and stand in each and every position on Lamade Field and try to imagine what a twelve-year-old must feel being surrounded by 40,000 plus fans during the championship game. I would also like to acknowledge Lance and his wife, Robin, for writing the book, PLAY BALL—The Story of Little League Baseball, which I read through seven times, giving me a substantial background on the history of Little League.

There are many other people at Little League deserving applause like Nora Haase, secretary to the president. Nora was my liaison who kept me up to date and in touch with Lance while my very first draft of a manuscript was being reviewed. Mike Miller heads up the Peter J. McGovern Museum.

Dottie Cox who ramrods the kitchen, Bonnie Lucas the head landscaper, Dave Fogel who operates the gift shop and Scott and Kathy Rosenberg were some of the other wonderful people who assisted me with information during my visit to Little League Headquarters.

Finally, I would like to thank the Valley Sports 2002 Little League team, their coaches, and the support of parents and Kentucky fans and businesses who during the year 2002 gave us all a memorable journey.

—LITTLE—
BIG
—MEN—

Foreword

My name is Bill Byham. I am a long-time fan of Little League Baseball and I have been very fortunate to sit behind a microphone to broadcast 42 consecutive Little League World Series. I have seen eleven-and twelve-year-old kids play this game in a most dramatic way before crowds of up to 40,000 fans.

I was there in 1971 when Gary, Indiana's Lloyd McClendon batted 1,000 by hitting five home runs in his five official times at bat. I was there in 1982 when Cody Webster of Kirkland, Washington, pitched and batted his USA team to a memorable 6-0 win over a team from Taiwan. I was there in 2002 when Aaron Alvey of the Valley Sports American team from Louisville, Kentucky, pitched and batted his team to a tense and thrilling 1-0 win over Sendai, Japan.

I also know Gary Yeagle and his family as neighbors in South Williamsport, Pennsylvania, where the world series is played every year.

In your hands, at this moment, is Gary Yeagle's written account of a team from Kentucky. The book starts with the team back home in Louisville and takes it all the way through an amazing run to become the Little League Baseball Champion of 2002.

I want you to know right up front in this introduction to *LITTLE BIG MEN: THE ROAD TO WILLIAMSPORT,* that the only person who could have written the book in this fashion is Gary Yeagle. He had lived the dream as a boy growing up in Williamsport, Pennsylvania, where Little League was founded by Carl Stotz in 1939. Gary played the game in his youth right where Carl Stotz originated the idea of baseball being played on a cut-down field so that young boys could learn and play the game.

What a thrill it was for Gary to go down to the ball field on a warm summer day and play the game on the field that Mr, Stotz had shaped for the young players. Gary says of his being a Little League baseball player, "Never the greatest, just one of the kids who came to the ball field with glove in hand, ready to give my best. It remains a most memorable time of my life."

At the time the Valley Sports team played in the World Series, the Yeagle family home was, and still is, located on the corner of East 7th Avenue in South Williamsport. Stepping out the front door of that house and walking just two short blocks takes anyone right into the area recognized around the world as Little League Village.

Because of that early youth in Williamsport, where he played the game and dreamed the dream Gary has never forgotten Little League baseball and the part it played in his own life. Each summer while living and working in Louisville, his thinking runs to the series when August shows up on the calendar and the world series qualifiers begin their drive toward Williamsport.

In was no different in August of 2002. In calls home to his mother, Margaret, better known to us as "Midge," he would talk of the coming series, never even thinking that a team from Louisville would become a team destined to reach the World Series, as well as to walk off the field as world champions.

He was going about his daily work in Louisville when the first whispers started about this Valley Sports American All-Star team. Where others in the community maybe caught a score in the paper, Gary Yeagle's interest carried that extra hope that the kids from his current home town in Kentucky could play their way into his old neighborhood in Pennsylvania.

As you know, it happened! You, the reader, will feel the pride of Gary Yeagle as he meshes his own history in Little League Baseball with the steps it took for the Valley Sports Little League team to write its history in becoming the World Champion in 2002. Enjoy!

—LITTLE—
BIG
—MEN—

Preface

LITTLE **BIG** MEN

In 1939, Carl E. Stotz founded Little League Baseball in the town of Williamsport, Pennsylvania. Today, it is the largest youth sports organization in the world. As a young boy growing up in Williamsport I had the privilege of not only playing on the diamond where the game was established, but also at the Original Field where the first twelve Little League World Series were played. The very first Little League team was Lycoming Dairy, and twenty years after their first game, I had the honor of playing third base for this team in 1959. In 2002, Valley Sports Little League team of Louisville, Kentucky, ventured on an incredible journey with a post-season record of 23-0 to win the 56th Little League World Championship. This is their story.

LITTLE
BIG
MEN

Growing Up In Williamsport

LITTLE BIG MEN

The early morning sun is just beginning to peek over the top of the Bald Eagle Mountain Range, with the sparkle of sunlight penetrating the forest, creating an awe-inspiring view of autumn color in North Central Pennsylvania. I'm standing in shallow center field, approximately twenty feet behind second base. Gazing over the well-manicured field of Kentucky Bluegrass, I contemplate how ironic it seems that the players who won the 2002 Little League World Series were from Kentucky. Valley Sports Little League situated in the southwest section of Louisville, Kentucky stood on this renowned field just two months ago as they were crowned champions of the world. Turning, I glance back toward the infield a few feet from first base as I recall Casey Jordan stabbing a hard line drive slammed by Japan's paramount hitter. That was it! The final out. Louisville, Kentucky–Valley Sports becomes the 56th team to achieve the honor of being the best Little League team in the world.

I've attended several Little League World Series events at Howard J. Lamade Stadium. My mother still to this day lives just two blocks from the 66-acre complex. This year, due to work schedules, my wife and I were unable to be present at the final game. This was rather frustrating for the both of us since we have lived in Louisville for a number of years, not to mention that I work about two miles from where the team played in Louisville.

We watched every game that Louisville played during the series, down in our family room as we surrounded ourselves with pretzels, favorite drinks and other assorted calorie-laden snacks. These were our boys, from our very own city and with each victory, we became even more enthused. The night of the World Series Championship we decided to head over to a local pub-restaurant and join in cheering the Valley Sports team to victory. The next morning my wife could hardly talk and remained hoarse for the rest of the week.

Yes, I've been here at Lamade Stadium when it comes down to the final out. Even though I wasn't here this year, I know exactly what it is like: players jumping up and down, overjoyed parents running onto the field, upwards of 40,000 excited and cheering fans. It's quiet here now. There's not a person to be seen. The stands are empty–there are no fans sitting out on the terraced grassy hills and no flashing cameras. It's so peaceful here at the moment almost as if the field is preparing for the next season.

When I think about what those twelve lads from Kentucky accomplished, it really is quite amazing. At the outset of the season, nearly 200,000 Little League teams, comprising more than 3 million little leaguers in over 100 countries on six continents, get the season under way. At the end of regulation play, the tournament process starts, which includes more than 37,000 games played over an eight-week period throughout the world. Only sixteen teams remain standing at the end of the two-month baseball formula of just not playing the game, but travel, discipline and remaining centered on the ultimate goal of getting to Williamsport. It reminds me of a large funnel, every game and team during the year thrown in, shuffled around and then, out of the narrow bottom, emerges just one team, the elite of the world.

Little League Baseball today is the largest youth sports organization in the world. As large as Little League is now, its very roots stem from a modest beginning. Approximately seven miles from this very playing field, on the north bank of the Susquehanna River, is where it all started.

In 1938, a native resident of Williamsport by the name of Carl E. Stotz gathered some neighborhood boys at a nearby field with hopes of starting up a baseball league for pre-teen children. With hardly any equipment and a handful of youngsters, Carl began to experiment with field dimensions, rules and regulations.

LITTLE BIG MEN

Carl began the search for sponsors in the spring of 1939 for his newly formed teams. Nearly fifty businesses turned him down. Refusing to give up, Carl talked with Lycoming Dairy, who agreed to go along and pay the $30 donation required to sponsor a team. Later that same year, Carl came up with two more advocates, Jumbo Pretzel and Lundy Lumber. On June 6, 1939, the first Little League game was played and the score was Lundy Lumber 23 and Lycoming Dairy 8. At the end of that first season, Carl set up a best of three games playoff between the two best teams. Lycoming Dairy, managed by Carl himself beat, Lundy Lumber three games to two, to go down in history as the first team to win the Little League Championship.

I wasn't born until 1946, and by that time, another field had been built just on the other side of Third Street. I was brought up on Memorial Avenue, just 500 yards from the 1939 playing field. During the summers of 1954, '55 and '56. I myself and most of the other neighborhood kids spent many a summer day playing ball on the very field where Little League came to be.

In 1965, I moved away from Williamsport, but each year I have returned to visit my parents. I'd drive around my 'ol stomping grounds and recall all of the magnificent moments that I experienced as a kid growing up in Williamsport. My favorite place to visit was and continues to this day to be that old ball field where we played baseball. A few years back, I noticed a monument had been built on the site. Upon close inspection, I discovered that the field we had played on as kids was actually where Little League was first introduced.

The day that I discovered the monument, I not only got out of my car to read the granite inscription but I went out onto the field. Nowadays the historic field is completely covered with grass. There is no backstop, base paths, dugout, not a thing other than that monument to indicate that baseball had ever been played there.

I remembered the field as it had been forty years ago. Back then it was more commonly referred to as a skin diamond. There wasn't a blade of grass in the infield—just dirt. I remember how we had to use sections of discarded cardboard or a smashed soda can to serve as one of the bases. I can still hear my mother when I would come home for supper after a day of playing ball on that desert of a field. She would always detour me before I had an opportunity to enter the house and direct me to the back porch where I received strict orders: "Gary Michael Yeagle, don't you even think of coming into this house with those clothes on. My Lord, son! Is there any dirt left on the field?"

We certainly had some great times on that old sand-lot field. There were days when I remember arriving at the field at the crack of dawn, and shortly afterward other kids would start to drop by. We'd play all morning long, taking a break at noon to dash up the street to the corner market for a cold soda and a bag of chips, then it was back to the field until supper time. And hour or so later, we'd return to the field and continue playing until it got too dark to see. When I think back, it seems that as kids growing up we were immortal. Following a day of pitching, hitting, running and sliding in that glorious dirt, we'd always return the next morning to go at it again.

We created some of the strangest rules ever developed. We never had enough kids to encompass nine players for both teams, so we always had to bend the rules. With as little as six players, we could conduct a ballgame on a full-size field. You had a pitcher, one infielder and an outfielder. If you hit a ball to the opposite field, you were automatically out. Three foul balls and you were out. You could be thrown out at the pitcher's mound instead of first base. The pitcher usually had to stand in as catcher for the opposing team on close

LITTLE **BIG** MEN

plays at home and on and on.

It was an all-day affair and as more kids showed up at the field the rules would change per the number of players. It was come one, come all. Kids would show up from other neighborhoods. Sometimes we didn't even know them, but they were welcome to play. Why, you didn't even need a glove, ball or bat to participate. There was always ample equipment to go around. If we didn't have at least six players, we'd spend the day just throwing the ball around or playing 500.

My fondest recollection of playing ball on that field was one afternoon when an ancient van pulled up next to the field. A man stepped out and waved to us, "Hey kids, com'n over here." We all ran from the field to the van where he opened the rear doors, exposing what appeared to be hundreds of Louisville Slugger baseball bats. You'd have thought we had discovered King Solomon's mines. To have a Louisville Slugger bat back then placed you right at the top of the pecking order. The man let us hold and swing various bats, then asked if we wanted to purchase one. Of course we wanted one of those bats–we just didn't have any money. He patiently waited while we each sprinted home to scrounge up what cash we could find. Ten minutes later, we all returned with a grand total of something less than three dollars. It wasn't nearly enough, but the man smiled and laughed, "Just enough. Pick one out, fellahs!"

That Louisville Slugger bat was like gold to us. There were five of us there that day. Each day one of the five would take the bat home and be responsible for its ultimate safe return the next day. I'll never forget the afternoon when that bat got broken for the first time. To this day I can't remember who it was that broke it, but I do recall that it was close to a public hanging. But, like most kids, we made the best of things and went on. That bat was nailed and taped together more times than I can recall. I bet it's still in someone's attic.

I have to smile when I think back to those days over four decades ago. We weren't old enough to play actual Little League ball, but we were learning and having a wonderful time. I think about how innocent we all were and how without any adult supervision we all got along. We played hard and abided by all the set rules, whatever they were for that particular day. We solved disagreements without any violence, treated each other with respect, regardless of race, belief or color, gave our best and never went home feeling dejected due to the outcome of the day on that old field.

In 1957, I walked over to Third Street and tried out for a Little League team at the Original League Field constructed in 1941. Unfortunately, I was not good enough to play on one of the teams. But that didn't mean that I didn't get to play. When Carl Stotz started to set up the original guidelines for Little League, he projected that as interest in the sport increased there would be many more children desiring to play than there were teams to accommodate them.

Carl built a farm team where kids could still get to participate and when a position opened up, then there was an opportunity for them to shift onto a regular team. In 1957, this farm team was referred to as the Morning League. My first year I spent my summer mornings playing third base, along with a bunch of other fellahs who weren't ready for Little League either.

I played on the Morning League for two years. I remember a conversation my coach had with me one morning after we lost a game. I'll never forget what he told me. Looking back now, I realize that he was only trying to coach me, but that day I went home with my tail tucked between my legs. He told me that I deserved to be on one of the regular Little League teams. I could catch the ball and throw, but I couldn't hit the ball. He had worked with me for hours on end, but for some reason, I couldn't hit a baseball to save my life. What seemed incredible is that when the neighborhood kids got together for a sand-lot game, I had no problem hitting the ball. There was just something about being in an actual game that made me freeze up.

In 1959, I finally made a team. I was chosen by Lycoming Dairy. That's right–one of the first three teams to ever play Little League Baseball. Twenty years after Carl Stotz put the program together and I'm playing third base for the first Little League team that came to be. I still couldn't hit. To this day, I don't know why they picked me. Maybe it was because it was my last year.

I played every game that season, stepped up to the plate two to three times each game and still didn't manage to get a single hit the entire season. One of my best friends, Jim, captured the 1958 batting championship. Then the year that I finally got to play third base, another close friend, Phil, acquired the '59 batting title. I was indeed surrounded by my pals who were great at the game, but I remained hitless.

Growing up like most kids, I had my idols in life. Mickey Mantle was at the top of my admiration list. Ol' Mick was and still is today one of the greatest home run hitters of all time. I wanted to be like him, to pound the ball like he did–to hit homers. Hitting a home run was part of Little League that I never got to relish. I couldn't even muster up a trivial single during the entire season, let alone hitting a home run.

I never got to watch the ball sweep over the outfield fence, with the opposing team standing there unable to do anything about it. I never got to circle the base paths, while my parents and neighbors cheered me on. I never crossed home plate, with my teammates huddling around me shouting, "Nice hit, great shot!"

Looking back now, as a young boy growing up in that 'ol neighborhood I was blessed. What a fabulous bunch of kids I grew up with! I can't remember one time when anyone remarked about what a terrible player I had been in Little League. It just wasn't an issue. I was their friend and that's all that mattered.

Yes, I grew up in Williamsport playing baseball. Growing up as a child, it was a way of life. Playing ball as a youth, I learned many valuable lessons, such as respect, fair play and, how to be a gracious loser. I often think about the Little League Pledge and, even today, I still have it memorized:

> *I trust in God. I love my country*
> *and will respect its laws. I will*
> *play fair and strive to win, but*
> *win or lose I will always do my best.*

I consider myself very fortunate to have grown up playing ball in Williamsport. Aside from being viewed as the mecca of Little League Baseball, Williamsport is no different than many communities across this nation and throughout the world where kids from all walks of life gather on numerous ball fields to play baseball with their childhood friends and dream of one day playing in the Little League World Series. Many teams have made the journey to Williamsport, but only 56 teams have made it to the finish line. In the year 2002, Valley Sports of Louisville, Kentucky, realized their dream. This is their journey–their story.

LITTLE BIG MEN

The Journey Begins

THE JOURNEY BEGINS

Once again, I'm standing in center field just a few yards behind second base. This field, like countless Little League fields around the world, appears identical in most aspects: Sixty feet between bases, forty-six feet from pitcher's mound to home plate, home and visiting team dugouts, an elevated announcer's booth, metal bleachers and an outfield fence painted with the names of local sponsors. What makes this playing field different is that it is the home of the 2002 Little League World Champions: Valley Sports of Louisville, Kentucky.

As I stand here in the middle of this field, I'm a bit overwhelmed when I ponder the reality that the Valley Sports' players started the regulation season right here on a field that, for lack of a better phrase, leaves me with a sense of utter humbleness. This is especially true when one considers that the closing game of the season played in Williamsport was in front of a crowd of close to 41,000 and viewed by approximately two million people.

There is a mystique that lingers around this particular ball field, despite the fact that there are only six groups of bleachers at the main field, seating around 240 local fans and parents. The infield grass is as green as I've seen anywhere, the outfield a little patchy, with a few mushrooms sprouting here and there and two of the sponsor billboards having fallen to the ground. But still, the young men who played ball on this very field accomplished what, at the beginning of the season, most folks would categorize as nearly impossible. These twelve players, with the guidance of three magnificent coaches and the support of numerous parents and local business owners, have handed Louisville yet another great sports topic that in my book rivals the rich history of Kentucky basketball and the Kentucky Derby.

Just as Little League Baseball has grown from a modest beginning, so has the Valley Sports Little League Organization. Just over forty years ago in

LITTLE BIG MEN

1961, in Louisville, Kentucky, a struggling Little League group on the edge of extinction searched for a field where they could play their ballgames. Authur Steilberg, a lumber and construction executive, stepped up to the plate and saved the day, donating a small plot of land consisting of seven acres behind his home. From 1961 until 1984, when Mr.Steilberg passed on, the league continued to utilize the field. In 1984, they moved to their present location between Pleasure Ridge Park High School and Greenwood Elementary School.

The league as it stands today has three playing fields, only one equipped with lighting. The league president and his staff have worked hard to enable Valley Sports to expand their facility, offering an opportunity for even more youngsters to play Little League.

During the 2002 regulation season, the players who made up the final Valley Sports' All-Star team, many who were rivals, probably couldn't have imagined that months later they would be world champions.

The journey the Valley Sports Little League took on the road to Williamsport, not to mention winning the World Series, is nothing less than amazing. It has been said that a journey can only be accomplished by taking the first step. The first step in this case was to assemble the roster. Prior to June 16th the coaches and team members were selected. Troy Osbourne, who coached a team called the Blue Jays to the regular season title, was made manager of the all-star team. Keith Elkins, who took the Astros to a second-place finish, also earned a position on the coaching staff. The third coaching slot was filled by Dan Roach, a gentleman who had been a coach and umpired in the league for a number of years.

Next, the process of putting the team together began as twelve players selected by their peers and coaches were announced:

Player . . . . Alex Hornback
Nickname . . . . Peanut
Born 11-7-90
Bats . . . . Right
Throws . . . . Right
Height . . . . 4'7"
Weight . . . . 79 lbs.
Jersey . . . . #2
Position . . . . Second Base
School . . . . St. Lawrence
Favorite Player . . . . Normar Garciaparra
Favorite Team . . . . Boston Red Sox

Player . . . . Shane Logsdon
Nickname . . . . Pudge
Born 6-16-90
Bats . . . . Right
Throws . . . . Right
Height . . . . 5'3"
Weight . . . . 130 lbs.
Jersey . . . . #16
Position . . . . Outfield-Pitcher
School . . . . Johnson Middle
Favorite Player . . . . Ken Griffey Jr.
Favorite Team . . . . Cincinnati Reds

LITTLE BIG MEN

Player . . . . Blaine Madden
Nickname . . . . Mad Dog
Born 1-9-90
Bats . . . . Right
Throws . . . . Right
Height . . . . 5'3"
Weight . . . . 126 lbs.
Jersey . . . . #8
Position . . . . Catcher-Outfield
School . . . . St. Paul
Favorite Player . . . . Javy Lopez
Favorite Team . . . . Atlantia Braves

Player . . . . Ethan Henry
Nickname . . . . EEEE
Born 11-16-89
Bats . . . . Right
Throws . . . . Right
Height . . . . 5'6"
Weight . . . . 131 lbs.
Jersey . . . . #19
Position . . . . Catcher
School . . . . Stuart Middle
Favorite Player . . . . Barry Bonds
Favorite Team . . . . New York Yankees

Player . . . . Zack Osbourne

Nickname . . . . Oz

Born 4-2-90

Bats . . . . Right

Throws . . . . Right

Height . . . . 5'4"

Weight . . . . 121 lbs.

Jersey . . . . #10

Position . . . . Pitcher-Shortstop

School . . . . St. Paul

Favorite Player . . . . Normar Garciaparra

Favorite Team . . . . Boston Red Sox

Player . . . . Wes Jenkins

Nickname . . . . Jynx

Born 2-13-90

Bats . . . . Right

Throws . . . . Right

Height . . . . 5'5"

Weight . . . . 130 lbs.

Jersey . . . . #18

Position . . . . Outfield

School . . . . St. Helen

Favorite Player . . . . Alex Rodriguez

Favorite Team . . . . Texas Rangers

LITTLE BIG MEN

Player . . . . Jake Remines
Nickname . . . . Max
Born 12-20-89
Bats . . . . Left
Throws . . . . Right
Height . . . . 5'5"
Weight . . . . 120 lbs.
Jersey . . . . #20
Position . . . . Outfield
School . . . . Stuart Middle
Favorite Player . . . . Jason Giambi
Favorite Team . . . . Atlanta Braves

Player . . . . Justin Elkins
Nickname . . . . Elk
Born 2-10-90
Bats . . . . Left
Throws . . . . Left
Height . . . . 5'2"
Weight . . . . 88 lbs.
Jersey . . . . #13
Position . . . . Outfield
School . . . . St. Polycarp
Favorite Player . . . . Ken Griffey Jr.
Favorite Team . . . . Arizona Diamondbacks

Player . . . . Aaron Alvey

Nickname . . . . Big A

Born 12-27-89

Bats . . . . Right

Throws . . . . Right

Height . . . . 5'7"

Weight . . . . 180 lbs.

Jersey . . . . #14

Position . . . . Pitcher-Outfield-SS

School . . . . Conway Middle

Favorite Player . . . . Derek Jeter

Favorite Team . . . . Cincinnati Reds

Player . . . . Josh Robinson

Nickname . . . . Jrob

Born 2-12-90

Bats . . . . Right

Throws . . . . Right

Height . . . . 5'3"

Weight . . . . 110 lbs.

Jersey . . . . #17

Position . . . . Third Base-Pitcher

School . . . . Conway Middle

Favorite Player . . . . Barry Bonds

Favorite Team . . . . San Francisco Giants

LITTLE BIG MEN

Player . . . . Casey Jordan
Nickname . . . . CJ
Born 10-30-89
Bats . . . . Right
Throws . . . . Right
Height . . . . 5'8"
Weight . . . . 145 lbs.
Jersey . . . . #22
Position . . . . First Base-Pitcher
School . . . . Farnsley Middle
Favorite Player . . . . Jason Giambi
Favorite Team . . . . Cincinnati Reds

Player . . . . Wes Walden
Nickname . . . . Waldo
Born 9-30-89
Bats . . . . Right
Throws . . . . Left
Height . . . . 5'6"
Weight . . . . 109 lbs.
Jersey . . . . #15
Position . . . . Outfield
School . . . . Conway Middle
Favorite Player . . . . Randy Johnson
Favorite Team . . . . Arizona Diamondback

Note: *Alex Hornback was added after the team was named due to a residential ruling on one of the initial players.*

The pieces of the puzzle had been gathered, but were by no means put together as became evident during their very first practice. The game plan from the beginning was that the team would succeed by means of pitching and defense, but another obstacle reared its ugly head: their defense bordered on horrible. Routine ground balls were getting through the infield, balls were falling in front of outfielders, the first baseman couldn't catch, and players couldn't make any good throws. During that initial practice, Dan Roach commented to Troy Osbourne, "This will never work."

The coaching staff had anticipated more from these twelve boys. They weren't new to the game. They were all-stars—they had played at Valley Sports for years and many of the players had been on the ten-year-old all-star team two years prior. The solution: was that the team wasn't allowed to pick up a bat for the first eight days of practice.

Defense became the word of the day as the team began to practice five hours per day during the week and up to eight hours on weekends. Defense was constantly preached and practiced repeatedly. But then, after nearly two weeks of practice, a monkey wrench was thrown into the gears as the team had to drop a player who was ruled ineligible due to residency requirements. A replacement player was needed before the team could move on. An eleven-year-old second baseman by the name of Alex Hornback was chosen and from the six regular season teams emerged the Valley Sports' All-Stars.

Now that Alex Hornback had been added to the team at second base, Josh Robinson moved to third base where he excelled. The outfielders, who during the regular season had been infielders were starting to get the hang of things. Zack Osbourne had shortstop down pat and eventually, Casey Jordan was installed at first base.

LITTLE BIG MEN

The long days of laborious practice continued, Troy teaching the boys grips and release points, Dan concentrating on the defense. Keith commented that each coach had a different style of teaching, but that all three worked well together. Dan was without a doubt the disciplinarian, making the players run when they screwed up, his previous military career definitely having an assertive influence on the team.

The players and the parents were in agreement that the lengthy workouts equaled nothing less than tense work—something that Valley Sports has always applied, resulting in a long history of success. The commitment to the players, combined with a basic work schedule, has regularly catapulted Valley Sports' regular season all-star teams deep into post-season play. Their six state championships are unequaled in the state of Kentucky. Considered a powerhouse as far as Little League Baseball is concerned, many teams in the region don't look forward to going up against Valley Sports.

Hats off to Arthur Steilberg whose generosity over four decades ago made it possible for a financially struggling Little League team, who was on the verge of folding, to continue to grow over the years and eventually gain the honor of Little League World Champions.

According to Keith Elkins, "It was fortunate how the team came together. Many teams develop internal problems but these kids had a method of working their problems out amongst themselves. The amazing thing about these boys…is that they matured very quickly."

Coach Dan Roach said, "We're not your ordinary Little League coaches. We put a lot of pressure on these kids."

The coaches' strict discipline was demanded on and off the field. The team was required to respond "Yes, sir," or "No, sir," when speaking with adults. They were required to conduct themselves with a high level of respect for those around them.

In watching this team play during the World Series playoffs, it was easy to see just how disciplined the team was. Sure, there were those moments of celebration following a great catch or a game winning hit, but there was no evidence of showboating, a lesson many professional athletes today could learn.

As June came to a close, Valley Sports was about to begin the journey as tournament play was about to start. Thousands of teams, not only from the United States but throughout the world, would begin the process of elimination. Elimination–a haunting word, especially when one considers just how difficult the road to Williamsport really is. Just to get to Williamsport, Valley Sports would have to win approximately seventeen games. There is little or no margin for mistakes along the way. Elimination always waits on the next pitch or play and within seconds the season can be ended.

Valley Sports was the 56th team to be crowned world champions, so this journey is by no means one of blazing a new path. It has been traveled by and conquered by fifty-five former teams–a long, hard journey, for not only the players and coaches, but for the parents as well. Let's take a quick snapshot at how the road to Williamsport is constructed–an incredible journey for those who survive.

The journey begins in late June as the regular season comes to a close, with leagues throughout the country and the world building all-star teams. A team can consist of as many as fourteen players between the ages of eleven and twelve on August 1st of the tournament year.

LITTLE BIG MEN

The initial round of tournament games begins around July 1st with district titles up for grabs. In the United States, district tournaments are played under the same rules, except for the location of the games. Some districts manage all the games at one site with the tournament host rotating on a yearly basis. Other districts utilize multiple locations with varying degrees of determination as to where the championship game is to be played.

Most district tournaments utilize a formula of double-elimination or Olympic-style pool play to determine the district champion, while other districts elect a single-elimination process. In many large districts, teams must compete in area tournaments, and then compete for the district trophy. Most district tournaments involve four to six teams. In the case of District 2 in which Valley Sports competes, there are eight teams in the district playoffs. Just to get through the initial level of tournament games, Valley Sports would have to gain six victories. This is no easy task since teams are pitted against some of the best players in their area.

Having acquired the prestige of district champion, teams in many larger states are required to advance to sectional play. In Kentucky, this is not the case. All the district winners enter the next level, which is the State Championship Tournament that normally starts at the end of July. The same rules that are applied to district play are identical during state playoffs. In the Kentucky State Championship Series, Valley Sports would be required to walk off with no less than five victories. The hazards are now even greater as teams go face-to-face with the best teams in their districts. When the state playoffs are finished, each state champion from the United States advance, to the next level along with the international teams.

The next level of competition comes in the form of the Regional Championship Tournament. In 2002, regional tournaments were played at five different sites throughout the United States, which includes eight regions of the country. States competing in each regional tournament are as follows:

- **Great Lakes Region** - Indianapolis, Indiana. State champions from Illinois, Indiana, Kentucky, Michigan, Ohio, and Wisconsin.
- **Mid-Atlantic Region** - Bristol, Connecticut. State champions from Delaware, the District of Columbia, New Jersey, Maryland, New York, and Pennsylvania.
- **Midwest Region** - Indianapolis, Indiana. State champions from Iowa, Nebraska, Minnesota, Missouri, Kansas, and North and South Dakota.
- **New England Region** - Bristol, Connecticut. State champions from Connecticut, Vermont, New Hampshire, Maine, Massachusetts, and Rhode Island.
- **Northwest Region** - San Bernardino, California. State champions from Idaho, Wyoming, Montana, Oregon, Washington, Hawaii, and Alaska .
- **Southeast Region** - St. Petersburg, Florida. State champions from Alabama, Florida, Georgia, North Carolina, South Carolina, Tennessee, Virginia, and West Virginia.
- **Southwest Region** - Waco, Texas. State champions from Arkansas, Colorado, New Mexico, Louisiana, Mississippi, Oklahoma, and East and West Texas.
- **Western Region** - San Bernardino, California. State champions from Utah, Nevada, Northern and Southern California, and Arizona.

Each regional location has playing and practice fields and living quarters for up to two-hundred players during the tournaments. In order for Kentucky to move on to the Little League World Series Tournament in Williamsport, they would have to knock off six state champions.

When the regional tournaments are finalized, aside from the eight United

LITTLE BIG MEN

States teams mentioned above, there are also eight international teams that are comprised of Canada, and the regions of the champions of Mexico, Asia, Caribbean, European, Latin American, the Pacific and Trans-Atlantic.

At this point, sixteen teams have accomplished what seems almost impossible. Over a two-month time frame, thousands of teams competing in more than 37,000 ballgames have dwindled down to these sixteen top teams. They have journeyed far and have endured much, but now the real test is about to begin. These players will face the best pitching they have ever seen, pitchers will do battle with some of the best hitters in the world, coaches will match their knowledge with the best in the business, and many parents who are worn out from traveling will make the final journey to Williamsport.

A word of apology may be necessary at this time as I realize that the last few pages are crammed with names, numbers, and locations, which may not have been that enjoyable to read but I wanted to inform those of you who are not that familiar with the structure of Little League to get a glimpse of just how tough this journey really is. It's more than just the World Series Championship Game or even the crucial two weeks of play. These players, these teams, have run the marathon, climbed the mountain, stayed the course to get to Williamsport, and then they are required to dig down even deeper in order to survive the last week of play.

Now that you have a better perception of what the journey entails, let's begin the adventure that the Valley Sports' players from Louisville, Kentucky started back in early July.

—LITTLE—
BIG
—MEN—

Coming Out of the Starting Blocks

LITTLE BIG MEN

Between 1962-64, I was on the Williamsport High School track team. One of the events I participated in was the 180-yard low hurdles. To this day, I'll never forget the sensation I felt the first day of competition–of competing not just against my fellow teammates, but against total strangers. I remember backing into the starting blocks at my first track meet. With my feet firmly placed into position my hands supporting me above the dirt, I looked up at the long cinder track ahead. It was time for the rubber to meet the road. It was all up to me now.

During those seconds before my first race, I wondered if I had trained hard enough–if I had done everything that I could. I recalled all those school mornings when I had gone down to the track and practiced before classes and the evenings I stayed after practice for a few more sprints. There was even a brief moment of humor when I remembered how I had confiscated a hurdle from the field and put in the alley behind my house so I could practice on weekends. There was no going back to the practice field for just one more sprint. The starting gun was only seconds from firing. I glanced at the runners on my right and left and wondered, *Am I as good as they are? Have they practiced as hard as I have? Is there something along the way that I have missed that could have made me better?* The clock was ticking and it was time for me to stop thinking about what I had to do. It was time to apply the training that I had received. There was no looking back.

In early July of 2002, Valley Sports stepped back into the starting blocks, so to speak. They had been drilled on every aspect of the game for days and hours on end. Now it was time to begin the district tournament. Would all of the intense training pay off? Would the regimentation of practicing the basics over and over net them with their first victory? It was time to test the waters. They had to be on top of their game. They were about to face some of the best teams in the city.

COMING OUT OF THE STARTING BLOCKS

Prior to their first district challenge, what type of thoughts raced through the minds of the twelve lads from Valley Sports? Would they be able to measure up to the all-stars of St. Matthews National who were to be their first district adversary; a section of the city who already had two state championships to their credit in 1991 and 1998? Had the players from St. Matthews trained as hard as they had? What kind of pitching would they be facing? Would they win their first game on the road to Williamsport?

When the dust settled following their first game, Valley Sports had come out on top with a decisive victory of 12-0. They had completely dominated the St. Matthews team. The plan the coaches had originally set of defense and pitching in order to win ballgames had a third dimension—these boys could hit and it seemed Valley Sports was running on all eight cylinders.

The second game facing Valley Sports was that of North Oldham. Any great concern the coaches may have had previous to the first game had to have been swept to the side with the lopsided victory over St. Matthews. It was evident that the grueling practice sessions had paid off. The Valley Sports' boys, with an enormous win beneath their belts, faced North Oldham head on and marched away with their second victory of 8-0. Their defense and pitching continued to confound their opponents, not to mention the fact that they were still hitting the ball.

With two games to their credit, Valley Sports prepared for the next game, but then something happened that dampened the spirit of the entire team. Brian Davis, without a doubt the team's most avid fan, died on July 3rd in a tragic motorcycle accident. Davis, 39, was present at just about every game at Valley Sports, even if his own sons were not playing. Employed by a local car dealership, it was said by friends that he only sold cars in between Little League games. He was so enthused about the team, always talking about how they were coming along.

Brian caught the baseball bug when his older son started playing and had coached both of his boys. As a twelve-year-old, one of his two sons was a member of a Valley Sports team that played in a regional tournament. From that moment on, Davis became adamant about Valley Sports making the trip to Williamsport.

As a point of record, he was so confident that after the district win over North Oldham, Brian predicted that Valley Sports would go to the Little League World Series. He called ahead and booked a room in Williamsport. Talk about faith in a team!

Brian enjoyed spending quality time with the players from Valley Sports, as he would invite team members over to his house for cookouts and some leisurely fishing in his pond. A friend of Brian's said that when he came back from that regional game, he was so fired up, saying, "We've just got to go there," meaning Williamsport.

At the viewing, many Valley Sports' players and coaches arrived wearing their team uniforms as they presented Melanie, Brian's wife, with an autographed baseball. Of her husband, Mrs. Davis said, "He was just so positive that they were going to go far…he talked about it all the time."

Despite this setback, the team had to continue on, no doubt with grieving hearts. They wore black wristbands displaying the initials, B. D. As the team ventured deeper into the district tournament, Brian Davis continued to be the topic of inspirational conversation:

"No matter what, Brian would have wanted them to keep on playing baseball—that was the inspiration the players had."

"It's funny that everyone's thinking the same thing. I bet Brian is up in heaven telling everyone, 'I told you so.'"

Each time the team made a great play, someone would comment, "You know Brian is smiling about that."

Valley Sports' third district game was against the all-star team from Camp Taylor. It must have been a difficult time for the players, coaches, and parents, as well. With the death of Brian Davis fresh on their minds, Valley Sports had to "get going" as the saying goes "when the going gets tough." Would their defense, great pitching and slugging continue?

The next day the box score in the paper clued us all in to the fact that Valley Sports was indeed still on the road to Williamsport, as they had taken Camp Taylor soundly—the final score 17-0. The team was not only running on all cylinders, but performing like a finely tuned machine. The first three games of the district playoff found Valley Sports undefeated by outscoring their opponents 37-0.

The next hurdle featured the team from Beuchel and the question was: Would Valley Sports continue their great run at the district title? In 1987, Beuchel had been state champs. The coaching staff never let up on the practice sessions that were just as regimented and tough as ever. Even though the team had competed wonderfully in their first three games, they were only at the halfway mark on their way to taking the tournament. The hurdle that the Buechel team represented was handled easily with yet another rout as they took out their fourth challenger by a score of 14-0, pushing their four-game run scoring total to a phenomenal 51-0.

LITTLE BIG MEN

When Valley Sports stepped onto the playing field just prior to their fifth district game, they had no idea that Jeffersontown, two-time state champs in 1988 and 1989 and one of the strongest leagues in the city, would slam the door on their "scoring-at-will" ability. Valley Sports managed to come away from this game with their fifth victory by a narrow margin of 2-1. The original agenda of defense and pitching had to fill the bill as the bats of the Valley Sports' squad had been silenced.

This game could have been one of disaster for the team. What if the final score would have been reversed, with Jeffersontown winning the game 2-1? It would have bordered on not only devastating, but quite unbelievable. Valley Sports could have been eliminated from district play even though they had a scoring run of 52-2. As I stated in the second chapter, there is little room for mistakes of any magnitude during the tournaments.

With their record situated at 5-0, Valley Sports was pitted in the district championship final once again against Jeffersontown for the title. Now, the team was faced with a different group of obstacles than they had before. They were going into the final tournament game undefeated, but they were facing a team who had played tougher than any of the other teams they had met.

The stage was set and the game was played. Valley Sports was back to its previous "bats in action" not to mention its ever-present great pitching and rock-solid defense. Valley Sports had knocked off Jeffersontown by a score of 8-0 and was standing tall as the District 2 Champion in Kentucky. The next stop on the journey would be the State Championship Tournament. The team would step into state competition with guns loaded. At this point, the team was 6-0, sporting a scoring marathon of 61-1, and averaging ten runs per game.

COMING OUT OF THE STARTING BLOCKS

The Valley Sports' All-Star team, selected just a few weeks prior to the district championship game, had been honed to be a team that was considered nothing less than dangerous when its members stepped onto a ball field. These twelve players who had been designated from six different teams came together as a single energetic team. When you compare how the Valley Sports team performed during its first practice sessions when the statement was made that, "This will never work!" to the stellar play they had produced during the district tournament, you really have to take your hat off to the coaching staff who, through long hours of practicing the basics, created a team of winners. Their system and method of training did work.

So, after the dust had cleared away, Valley Sports of Louisville reigned as District 2 champs. In other areas of the state, seven other district champions had clawed their way through district playoffs and would be off to the state championship tournament. Below are the results of the district tournaments held in Kentucky:

District 1 Champion–Owensboro Southern
District 2 Champion–Valley Sports
District 3 Champion–Richmond National
District 4 Champion–Clay County
District 5 Champion–Campbellsville Youth Baseball
District 6 Champion–Morehead
District 7 Champion–Pikeville
District 3 Runner Up–Winchester National

LITTLE **BIG** MEN

In the five other states that make up the Great Lakes Region, of which Kentucky is a part, district champions were named:

Illinois

District 7 Champion–Evergreen Park
District 10 Champion–River Forest
District 15 Champion–Clear Ridge
District 17 Champion–Macomb
District 18 Champion–Bradley-Bourbonnais American

Indiana

District 2 Champion–Munster American
District 4 Champion–West Terre Haute
District 6 Champion–New Castle
District 8 Champion–Brownsburg
District 10 Champion–Georgetown National-Ft. Wayne
District 11 Champion–South Bend Southwest
District 12 Champion–Seymour
District 14 Champion–Warsaw

Michigan

District 1 Champion–Midland Northwest
District 2 Champion–Eastwood
District 3 Champion–Blissfield
District 4 Champion–Birmingham
District 5 Champion–Lincoln Park American
District 6 Champion–Grosse Pointe Farms-City
District 7 Champion–Richmond
District 8 Champion–Traverse City East
District 9 Champion–Georgetown National-Jennison

District 10 Champion–Escanaba
District 11 Champion–Negaunee
District 12 Champion–Roosevelt Park
District 13 Champion–Petosky
District 14 Champion–Bay City East
District 15 Champion–Dowagiac

Ohio

District 1 Champion–Eastlake
District 2 Champion–Canfield
District 3 Champion–Cuyahoga Falls North
District 4 Champion–Holmes County West-Lakeville
District 5 Champion–Cambridge
District 7 Champion–New London
District 8 Champion–Patterson Park-Dayton
District 9 Champion–Hamilton West Side American
District 10 Champion–Maumee
District 11 Champion–Ironton

Wisconsin

District 1 Champion–West Bend American
District 2 Champion–Appleton Lyons
District 3 Champion–Eau Claire American
District 4 Champion–Madison Kennedy
District 5 Champion–Merrill
District 6 Champion–Lakeland National-Salem

The battle lines for the Kentucky State Little League Tournament had been drawn, not to mention state tournaments for the other states in the Great Lakes Region. Part one of the Little League International Tournament had come to an end. Every state across the United States would now venture into phase two with state titles up for grabs. Aside from the Great Lakes Region, seven other regions in the United States and eight international regions were beginning the process of elimination as district and sectional champions were named throughout the world.

Valley Sports, with little doubt, had blasted out of the starting blocks. They had jumped six hurdles during district play with a phenomenal performance. The training that the coaches constantly demanded was evident when you consider the results.

With the district championship title in their hip pocket, it was back to the drawing board since the state tournament would not be played until late July. The regimented five-hour weekday practice sessions and weekend workouts would continue. Valley Sports could not rest on their laurels. If the players expected to win the state title, they would have to turn the intensity up a notch as they would face off with the best players in the state of Kentucky.

—LITTLE—
BIG
—M E N—

Going for Number Six

LITTLE BIG MEN

The heat of July in Kentucky set in as the state playoffs were about to begin at Lykens Park in Winchester, Kentucky. Between the time that the district tournament ended and the state playoffs began, the coaching staff of Valley Sports continued to drill the team. To a lot of people, the state tournament might have seemed like just another sequence of baseball games to determine the state champion, but it was much more than that.

This was the second step of three that Valley Sports had to deal with if the team expected to get to Williamsport. True, the team was taking an impressive district performance into the state playoffs, but now the players and teams it would face were the best in the state: seven other teams who had their sights set on getting to the Little League World Series.

Bringing state championships home was nothing new for Valley Sports' teams. Going into the 2002 season they had gained the state title five times, an accomplishment that is unprecedented in the state of Kentucky. The first championship came back in 1968 and then they remained silent until they won three titles back-to-back in 1994, 1995, and 1996. The last title came in 1999. So, winning the state championship was by no means new ground to Valley Sports. Even though the team carried an unequaled record of state victories into the 2002 tournament, this was just a matter of bygone history. If the team expected to be left standing at the last game of the state tournament, it would have to buckle down and continue their proven pattern of pitching, hitting, and defense.

The Kentucky State Tournament is divided into two separate four-team groups. After round-robin pool play, the top two teams from each division advance to single-elimination in semifinal and championship games. On the next page are the Pool A and Pool B teams for 2002:

GOING FOR NUMBER SIX

Pool A Teams	Pool B Teams
Owensboro Southern	Richmond National
Valley Sports-Louisville	Campbellsville Youth
Clay County	Pikeville
Morehead	Winchester National

On Saturday July 20th, which was the first day of tournament play, Valley Sports faced Clay County. In the first inning, the players from Louisville came out swinging, scoring two runs on three hits and two passed balls, a double by Zack Osbourne and singles by Jake Remines and Casey Jordan. In the bottom of the first, Clay County went down swinging as Josh Robinson struck out the side. The single run that Clay County produced was a home run during the second inning.

Valley Sports smashed the game wide open in the sixth on singles from Wes Jenkins, Aaron Alvey, Osbourne and Remines. These four base hits combined with four wild pitches caused Valley Sports to walk away with its first victory at the state tournament with a final score of 7-1.

Valley Sports hadn't missed a single beat as the players picked up right where they had left off at district play earlier in July. Their pitching stood as topnotch, Robinson and Alvey combining for thirteen strikeouts. Their bats were singing again as the team collected eight hits. The team was now 7-0 in tournament play and one step closer to Williamsport. In other games, Owensboro Southern defeated Morehead, Richmond National beat Winchester National, and Campbellsville Youth claimed a win over Pikeville.

The second day of the tournament gained Owensboro Southern and Campbellsville their second victories over Clay County and Winchester National, while Richmond handed Pikeville its second defeat. Valley Sports also picked up a second win against Morehead by a sheer margin of 1-0 on a late home run in the sixth inning by Osbourne. Jordan had hit two singles and Alex Hornback a hit, but they had been stranded on base. The bats of Valley Sports had been silenced once again. However, Alvey had pitched a great game, tossing a no-hitter and striking out nine batters along the way. Their defense was impeccable as usual.

The third day of the state tournament went into the history books as Clay County defeated Morehead, Winchester National gained a victory over Pikeville, and Campbellsville picked up its third victory against Richmond National. Valley Sports also won its third game over Owensboro Southern in a game that was insignificant since both teams had already earned a berth in the semifinals.

After the standard six innings of play, Valley Sports and Owensboro were deadlocked in a 4-4 tie. The game continued on for eight more innings until finally in the top of the fourteenth at 1:30 in the morning, Shane Logsdon hit a double followed by a sacrifice bunt by Hornback and an intentional walk handed to Osbourne when Blaine Madden finished the game with two RBI's. The final score–Valley Sports defeated Owensboro 6-4.

Even though the team had logged its third victory in the tournament, the coaches felt that they hadn't prepared themselves for the game. They had to go heavy into their lineup using six different pitchers–a situation they had not previously experienced. Coach Dan Roach said the team was a little too cocky and there was too much clowning around. The following day while Winchester National and Campbellsville were picking up wins over Pikeville and Richmond National, Valley Sports not only received a hardy discussion but a lengthy practice. Surprisingly, the four runs that Owensboro Southern scored in this game were to be the most runs allowed by Valley Sports during the entire post-season tournaments: it had been a wake-up call.

The regulation pool play was over and the semifinals were about to start. The team standings at this point were as follows:

Pool A Standings	W	L
Valley Sports	3	0
Owensboro Southern	2	1
Clay County	1	2
Morehead	0	3

Pool B Standings	W	L
Campbellsville Youth	3	0
Richmond National	2	1
Winchester National	1	2
Pikeville	0	3

On July 24th, the semifinals started as Owensboro Southern took on the undefeated team from Campbellsville and Valley Sports braved the Richmond National team. Valley Sports, after just the first inning, had proven once again that it was indeed a powerhouse. Singles hit by Remines, Robinson, and Hornback and home runs by Alvey and Osbourne gave Valley Sports a 10-0 lead as the first inning came to a close. Aside from the hitting clinic that Valley Sports put on, Richmond National's defense and pitching had fallen apart with two fielding and three throwing errors, two walks, and two wild pitches.

In the second inning, Valley Sports grabbed its eleventh run as Jordan and Robinson combined for two singles. The game finally ended with the scoreboard displaying the end result. Valley Sports had won its fourth state

LITTLE BIG MEN

championship game at 11-0. The state championship final was primed as Owensboro had beaten the undefeated Campbellsville team.

Following the extra inning game with the Owensboro team, Valley Sports was once again right on target with great pitching, awesome defense, and run-scoring ability. The team would now enter the last game with a record of 10-0, outscoring its opponents by an amazing 86-6.

The Owensboro Southern team had its work cut out as its final competitor was the only team who had defeated them during the tournament. Valley Sports, on the other hand, could not view the Owensboro team lightly as they had done on their first meeting during the fourteen-inning marathon earlier in the week.

On July 25th, precisely one month prior to the Little League World Series Championship Game, Owensboro Southern and Valley Sports stepped onto the field to do battle, not only for the Kentucky State Championship, but also for the honor of representing Kentucky in the Great Lakes Regional Tournament. This would be the final phrase of playoff games before those teams still left standing would travel to Williamsport.

Aaron Alvey, one of Valley Sport's two strongest pitchers, stood on the mound, with Ethan Henry behind the plate. The team was indeed ready for this final game and in the first inning the players managed to get their first run on a walk by Osbourne, a sacrifice bunt laid down by Remines, followed by Alvey's single enabling Osbourne to cross the plate.

The score remained at 1-0 until the fourth inning when Henry hit a double to left-center field. Going to third on a passed ball, Henry scored due to a throwing error by Owensboro. The score at the end of four innings, was

42

2-0, with Valley Sports slightly increasing their slim lead.

In the sixth inning, Valley Sports would score what was to be the final run of the game as Henry smacked one out of the park. The team's lead was now at 3-0, which turned out to be the final tally. Valley Sports was now officially the 2002 Kentucky State Champion, setting yet another benchmark for future teams as they grabbed their sixth state title.

The final outcome of the 2002 Kentucky State Championship went into the record books:

Team	W	L
Valley Sports	5	0
Campbellsville	3	1
Owensboro Southern	3	2
Richmond National	2	2
Clay County	1	2
Winchester National	1	2
Morehead	0	3
Pikeville	0	3

In analyzing the state championship tournament, some very interesting facts surface, indicating that despite the actuality that Valley Sports could not only hit the ball and produce runs, they still finished third place in batting percentage behind Campbellsville and Owensboro, as shown on page 44:

LITTLE BIG MEN

	Campbellsville	Owensboro	Valley Sports
Average	.418	.287	.259
Runs	32	31	28
Hits	38	39	36
Doubles	8	10	5
Triples	2	1	0
Home Runs	2	2	5

The statistics above indicate that Campbellsville and Owensboro had hit more effectively than Valley Sports during the tournament. So why did Valley Sports seize the title? Great pitching and strong defensive finesse had shut down the bats of Owensboro. Fortunately, Valley Sports didn't get an opportunity to play Campbellsville since they had been defeated by Owensboro. The hitting and scoring talent that the two best batting percentage teams generated was only apparent when they were up against other teams in the tournament. We'll never know what might have happened if Valley Sports and Campbellsville had met for the state championship game.

In the pitching category, Valley Sports was at the top of the list with the lowest earned-run average (ERA) of the tournament, coming in at 0.50, considerably less than the second place team, which was Owensboro with a 1.54 ERA. Again, one of the two factors the Valley Sports' coaches said would carry them through becomes evident–great pitching!

When you look at the ten best pitchers during the tournament, it's easy to see why Valley Sports walked away with the state title. Aaron Alvey topped the list, with Zack Osbourne and Wes Jenkins taking the third and fourth place slots. Wes Walden came in at the sixth position and, finally, Shane Logsdon filled the eighth spot. This was more proof that great pitching was a vital key to Valley Sports' success.

In the defensive category, where they had worked so diligently, Valley Sports captured third-place honors. Team members had committed seven errors but their ability to gain runs when needed had balanced the fielding mistakes they made.

Hitting the ball had become an added feature to the Valley Sports team. When you consider that close to 96 young men were involved in the state tournament, the following stats are impressive:

Hits–Zack Osbourne finished first with eight hits while Aaron Alvey tied for second with seven hits.

Runs Scored–Zack Osbourne gained second place with eight runs scored.

Runs Batted In–Zack Osbourne captured the first position with eight RBIs and Aaron Alvey nailed a tie for third place with six RBIs.

Total Bases–Zack Osbourne took the honors in this category with a first place total of nineteen, while Aaron Alvey tied for third with eleven.

Home Runs–Zack Osbourne rose to the top with a total of three homers.

Of the top twenty-five hitting players the following were from Valley Sports in the state tournament:

Player	Avg.	Top 25 position
Zack Osbourne	.615	4th
Alex Hornback	.417	16th
Aaron Alvey	.368	22nd
Casey Jordan	.333	25th

Note: In the second chapter, I wrote that the team had to pick up a new player since one of the original players selected was ruled ineligible to play. That new player was Alex Hornback, a 4'7" eleven-year-old second baseman. Hornback was chosen because the coaching staff was of the opinion that Alex could handle ground balls. Alex's presence not only helped to fortify the defense, but he turned out to be a tough out at the plate. Alex Hornback was by no means the single success story on the Valley Sports team–and I say team because that is the very reason why at this point during tournament games that they remained undefeated at 11-0. You just never knew who was going to get that hit or who was going to make a great play.

Next stop: Great Lakes Regional Tournament scheduled to begin on August 3, 2002, less than two weeks away. Brian Davis would have been proud.

—LITTLE—
BIG
—M E N—

The Ladder of Success

LITTLE BIG MEN

My senior year at Williamsport High School, just two months prior to graduation, I remember a particular history lesson when the teacher decided rather than speaking about events of the past he was going to tell us about the future and how we would get there. He told us that we would soon all graduate–that each one of us would be going in a different direction in our lives.

Some would be heading to college, while others would join the military and still others seeking employment at various jobs. However, he commented that it made no difference what our individual goals in life were—we all, each and every one, would have to climb the ladder of success to attain them.

His description of this ladder of success was not exactly what I would refer to as very enlightening. According to him, the ladder had been climbed by literally countless people in the past. It was not an easy climb. Many of the rungs had been stepped on so many times that they could easily break, causing an individual to plummet back to the ground. He felt that in life there are few people who will catch you as you fall. As a matter of fact, most people have a tendency to move to the side, watch you as you descend helplessly, and then step up a rung to take your place. Another choice example he gave us was if someone was just below you, more than likely he would not be open to the idea of pushing you up higher. Instead he might try to actually shove you out of the way so that he could move up.

I left class that day thinking about this long ladder that I was about to climb. That night at home while discussing this "ladder business" with my dad, he agreed with my history teacher, saying that the ladder simply represented life, which by no means was easy and if I took the time to think about it, I had already been on the ladder many times as a boy growing up. The ladder was not exclusively for adults. Smiling, he told me not to be too concerned with climbing this ladder of success, but to concentrate on the ladder of faith.

You may be asking yourself what this smidgen of wisdom has to do with Little League Baseball or the Valley Sports Little League team. The point is— my father was right. As a young fellah growing up like most youngsters, I was always on that ladder trying my best to learn something new or just trying to improve myself.

Valley Sports stepped up onto that very first rung of the Little League World Series ladder when their all-star team was formed. There were thousands of teams crowded on that bottom rung, all geared on moving up during district play. Only one team from each district would make it to the top of the district ladder. The same thing can be said of the state championships, as well. Only one select team from each state arrives at that level of height on the ladder.

Valley Sports was prepared to climb toward the eventual goal on the ladder–the regional championship. As on most ladders, the higher you climb, the more formidable it can become. At this point of tournament play, the rungs on the ladder had broken out under many teams as they had been eliminated from moving up. So far, except for two very close games, the climb for Valley Sports appeared to be rather easy. But now they were about to challenge five other state champions, teams that had worked their way up the ladder, as well.

On August 3, 2002, in Indianapolis, Indiana, the Great Lakes Regional Tournament would get under way. The games would be played at Stokley Field, Reuben F. Glick Little League Center. Participants are listed on page 50:

LITTLE BIG MEN

Michigan State Champion
Grosse Pointe Farms-City Little League
Grosse Pointe Farms, Michigan

Indiana State Champion
Brownsburg Little League
Brownsburg, Indiana

Wisconsin State Champion
Merrill Little League
Merrill, Wisconsin

Ohio State Champion
West Side American Little League
Hamilton, Ohio

Illinois State Champion
Bradley-Bourbonnais American Little League
Bradley-Bourbonnais, Illinois

Kentucky State Champion
Valley Sports Little League
Louisville, Kentucky

On Saturday, the all-star team of Brownsburg, a two-time Great Lakes Regional Champion in 1999 and 2000, defeated Wisconsin's Merrill team by a score of 6-1. Later that night, Valley Sports took on the Ohio State Champion who also had won the Great Lakes Regional two times in 1991 and 1993. Kentucky defeated the Hamilton West Side team by a margin of 5-0, with their pitching and defense preventing the team from Ohio from accruing a single run. Valley Sports had boosted their tournament record to 12-0. The five runs Valley Sports managed to push across the plate were well below their average of eight runs per game, but it was enough to get the job done.

The next day, Sunday, Kentucky had the day off as far as tournament play was concerned. Two other important contests were played as Grosse Pointe Farms from Michigan was defeated by Ohio with a score of 9-7. In the night game, Bradley-Bourbonnais of Illinois handed Wisconsin their second defeat of the tournament with a score of 10-3.

Monday at 12:30 p.m., Kentucky was again in action as the team battled the Illinois State Champion. Valley Sports picked up their second win of the tournament, but with somewhat less flair than they had been accustomed. The final score of 2-1 indicated that Valley Sports was still pitching well, with their defense holding firm, but their ability to score an average of eight runs per game had not been evident. Even though the team now held a record of 13-0, they had dodged another bullet. That night, another game took place as the Michigan State Champions beat the team from Indiana by 6-0.

During Tuesday's, afternoon event, Kentucky defeated Wisconsin by a score of 4-1, not only picking up their third victory of the tournament, but handing Merrill their third loss. Valley Sports' pitching and defense had once again shut down their opponent, but their hitting had only gained them four runs. Even though it had been enough to push their winning tally to 14-0, it appeared that ever since starting regional play, big margin victories had disappeared. The other main game played that evening pitted Brownsburg against Hamilton West Side, the only two teams that had previously won the regional title and made the trip to Williamsport. As the dust settled, Indiana was the victor, with Ohio suffering their second loss at 5-4.

LITTLE BIG MEN

The next day of competition found Valley Sports with a day off. In games played that day, Illinois handed Michigan its second defeat with a score of 5-2, while in the late game, Hamilton West Side won over the Wisconsin team by 9-2.

Thursday, August 8th, Illinois faced Indiana in the first game. Brownsburg shut out the Bradley team 2-0. At 6 p.m., Kentucky was matched against the Michigan team. Valley Sports strolled away with its fourth win of the tournament with a score of 3-1, which was another game where pitching and defense had saved the day. Compared to the eleven games that Valley Sports had taken in the districts and states, its scoring now had to be considered mediocre. Their record was 15-0, nothing to sneeze at. They were winning games with superb pitching and great defense, but their hitting had fallen off drastically. This had to be a great concern for the entire team. Sooner or later, they were bound to run up against a team that could hit their pitching.

On Friday, August 9th, the semifinals were about to get started, with two night games on tap. The first game was between Indiana's Brownsburg team and the Bradley-Bourbonnais squad from Illinois. Indiana fought its way into the regional championship game with a slim 2-0 victory over the Illinois team, guaranteeing them a shot at a third regional title.

In the 8:15 game, Kentucky got ready to face the Hamilton West Side team. The game was scoreless until the fourth inning when Hamilton put together an error and a double to grab the early lead. Kentucky was kept at bay with just three hits, until the bottom half of the fourth, when they tied the game at 1-1, Josh Robinson scored following a double by Osbourne. Zack, then struck out the side in the fifth and sixth innings. In the sixth, Ethan Henry got to first base on a walk. The next batter struck out as Henry advanced to second on a passed ball. Justin Elkins, a late-inning replacement, stepped up to the plate and hit the third pitch down the first base line where it bounced off Hamilton's first baseman out into the outfield, scoring Henry from second to win the game 2-1. Kentucky won yet another game by the skin of their teeth.

Saturday, August 10th, the biggest day yet for Valley Sports was set to begin. The championship game in Indianapolis represented the final hurdle the team from Kentucky had to overcome. The finish line was in sight–just six innings away. The ultimate goal of getting to Williamsport was within their reach–just one more game! You have to wonder what kind of thoughts were going on inside the minds of the players. Were they nervous? After all, they were going up against a team that was the defending Great Lakes Champion. Were they concerned about the truth that ever since they had started regional competition that they were not hitting the ball like they had during district and state play? They were so close to making the trip to Pennsylvania. Had they come this far only to fall at the last moment?

To tell the truth, I think that the coaches, parents and fans may have considered these matters. But as for the players, well, they are just kids. If I can remember myself as a twelve-year-old the outcome of any day was of no great concern to me. I always did my best, but whatever the outcome was–I still had fun. This is an important message for all of us as adults. We want our children to win, to do well, to make us all proud. But we must be careful not to place unbearable pressure on children; there's time enough for that when they become adults.

So, the question remains: What did the players from Valley Sports think as they stood on Stokley Field? They had everything going for them: A 16-0 record, a great coaching staff, phenomenal pitching and defense, fan support

LITTLE BIG MEN

and one other thing. This team had Brian Davis smiling down from above, and I can't help but think that Valley Sports had been blessed ever since the moment Brian booked that room in Williamsport.

At 8:15, the game kicked off. The game was televised by ESPN2 and the excitement in Louisville was not just limited to the area where Valley Sports had played, but spread throughout the city. To make a long story short, Valley Sports had returned to its old habit of combining not only pitching and defense, but hitting, as well. Aaron Alvey, on the mound, pitched a fourteen-strikeout game, limiting Brownsburg to just four hits and one run.

Three of Brownburg's four hits came in the very first inning in the style of singles, but they were unable to score, with Alvey striking out the side. The kids from Louisville hitched together eight runs, winning the Great Lakes Regional Tournament by a score of 8-1. The dream was now reality. Next stop Williamsport and the Little League World Series.

Brian Davis was never very far from the minds of the players. Manager Troy Osbourne motioned for Melanie Davis to come down from the stands onto the field where she was presented with a framed team photograph with the inscription near the bottom: *In memory of Brian Davis, our angel in the outfield.*

When I think back to those words of wisdom my father gave me in high school of not being that concerned about climbing the ladder of success, but to concentrate on the ladder of faith, it seems to me that this team of young Little Leaguers from Louisville, Kentucky, did just that! It's obvious that the coaches had enormous faith in these boys, not to mention the support of the parents. But, despite all the faith and great support, each player still had to perform, and perform they did. You just never knew who was going to make the next great defensive play or who was going to get that vital hit.

At the start of tournament play, the coaches were of the opinion that between the pitching of Alvey and the defense of Osbourne that they could go a long way. Each and every player of Valley Sports had at one moment or another "stepped up to the plate" and met the challenge doing what they could to contribute to their undefeated record. Let's take a look at the individual players and see some of the great contributions that carried this team not only through district and state championships, but the regional title as well:

Alex Hornback–Carried a batting average of .350 during the state and regional tournaments.

Blaine Madden–Banged a game winning single in the top of the 14th to defeat Owensboro Southern during the state tournament.

Ethan Henry–Held a batting average of .455, scoring four runs in the regional tournament.

Zack Osbourne–Batted .612 in the state and regional tournaments and won two games in the regionals as a pitcher.

Shane Logsdon–Pitched four scoreless innings during the regional tournament.

Justin Elkins–Slammed a two-out single in the bottom of the sixth inning in the regional semifinals against Ohio to win the game 2-1 and keep the dream alive.

Aaron Alvey–Struck out fourteen batters in the regional championship game, catapulting the team toward Williamsport.

Wes Walden–Scored a run and walked in four plate appearances during the regionals.

Josh Robinson–Struck out three batters in a row in regional play.

LITTLE BIG MEN

Wes Jenkins–Contributed with a valuable RBI during the regional tournament.

Casey Jordan–Gained a pitching victory at the regionals allowing no earned runs.

Jake Remines–Hit .333 during state and regional play.

These are but a few of the commendable contributions these young men made toward the success of the team. Some of these instances may seem to be rather unimportant, but each event is equally important when you consider that they played as a team, not individuals. Remember what I said in the second chapter about the team being a large puzzle. True, some players at times may appear to be a larger part of the puzzle, but the entire puzzle can never be completed until every *piece* is in place.

I think the most amazing aspect about Valley Sports reaching their goal of going to Williamsport is that they are such a small organization. Back in June when the team was formed, the coaching staff had to choose from approximately thirty eligible players from six teams. Who would have thought that this group of players who at the beginning of the journey couldn't field, throw or catch, according to their coaches, would go all the way through district, state and regional tournament games, reaching their ultimate goal of getting to Williamsport. Brian Davis thought they could do it–and indeed they did! Valley Sports of Louisville, Kentucky, practiced and played their hearts out as they ventured on the incredible journey. They had indeed come out of the starting blocks and climbed the ladder of success with faith.

LITTLE BIG MEN

The Promised Land

LITTLE BIG MEN

As a general rule, I don't read the paper, watch television or listen to the radio that much, so by the time Valley Sports was preparing to journey to Williamsport I was totally unaware that a team from the Louisville area was even in the Little League World Series Tournament. My first clue as to the success of this team occurred one morning on my way to work when I noticed a sign on the front of a local business as I drove down Dixie Highway: VALLEY SPORTS–NEXT STOP WILLIAMSPORT.

It wasn't so much that I recognized the Valley Sport's name, but more that of Williamsport, the community where I had grown up as a young boy. I figured the sign had something to do with Little League Baseball since it was that time of the year, but who was Valley Sports?

Arriving at work, I started to ask around and my fellow employees, most of whom were from the area where the players from Valley Sports lived were quick to fill me in on the team's incredible series through district, state and regional playoff games. Now they were going to Williamsport to play in the Little League World Series Tournament.

During mixed conversations when I brought up the fact that I had been raised in Williamsport and played baseball not only on the ball field where it had all started back in 1939, but had actually been on a team at the original stadium where the championship had been played from 1947-58, there were many questions. What's Williamsport like? Is the stadium big? Where is Williamsport and on and on?

My answer to these questions was that Williamsport is no different than many communities across the country. There are shopping centers, grocery stores, dry cleaners, car washes, churches and most of the things one would find in any town. As for the field–well, it's nothing short of immaculate; as clean and well-maintained as any major league field. Where is Williamsport? Nestled in the peaceful hillsides of the Bald Eagle Mountain Range of North Central Pennsylvania. Williamsport is a very normal town, except for two weeks in late August when sixteen teams, not only from the United States, but from around the world, travel to this town in the mountains, the promised land–the land of milk and honey.

Growing up in Williamsport, I didn't feel as if I were living in a town that held a carnival atmosphere or a Disney-effect on the people who live there. But during that two-week period, when Little League kicks in, there is an unseen magical cloud that hangs over the surrounding area, especially for the teams who arrive at this much-desired field. For them, it probably does seem like the promised land.

The sixty-plus-acre property definitely has it all when it comes to Little League Baseball. I remember when I had moved back to Williamsport years ago with the corporation where I worked. I had been away from home, except for a yearly vacation, for nearly thirty years. I was only a return resident for four years when I finally relocated in Louisville, Kentucky, but during the tournament in August, I spent every moment I could watching the games during the series.

Prior to the semifinals, its not as crowded and I found it quite amazing to be able to walk over to the field, purchase a hot dog and soda for less than a $1.50, then stroll in and watch the game without being charged an admission fee. I often find myself comparing this scenario with that of major league baseball, where it can cost the average Joe a week's earnings just to take his family out to attend a ballgame.

Yeah, I'd have to state that during the Little League World Series Playoffs

LITTLE BIG MEN

that Williamsport is the promised land. Years ago when I lived there, I was attending a game mid-week. I was seated out on the grassy hill in center field next to group of parents from Hawaii who had a team in the playoffs. In the course of a conversation that I had with one of the fathers, I told him that I couldn't believe that he was actually from Hawaii. My wife and I always wanted to go there and we never really had had the opportunity. The man gave me the strangest look as he said, "But you live here in Williamsport, the birthplace of Little League…why, just look at that wonderful field and the mountains. As far as I'm concerned and no doubt the rest of the parents and kids on our team, this is the land of milk and honey–the promised land!"

I suppose that's the way of most communities. If you happen to live in a town where there is an event or something of great interest, it can and often does become old hat or commonplace to those who live there. For example, I have resided in Louisville for nearly eighteen years now and in all that time, I have only gone to the Kentucky Derby one time. Just this past year, my wife and I were on vacation in South Carolina. I met some folks from Georgia while walking on the beach. When they discovered that I was from Louisville, they asked me about the Derby. When they found out that I had only been to one race, they were amazed, commenting that if they lived there they would go every year.

So, what do the teams who get to go to Williamsport during tournament play think when they first arrive at the stadium that exemplifies the high point of Little League Baseball? For the teams who have made the journey to Williamsport, it must be an uncanny glimpse and experience. Howard J. Lamade Stadium can seat nearly 45,000, including the grassy hillside surrounding the outfield. Little League Headquarters and the museum are up on the hill a little farther, where one can not only behold, but experience, the past history of Little League. To the right of the stadium, nestled in a grove of trees, is the housing for the teams, complete with a large swimming pool, ping pong tables, and all of the other amenities required for a home away from home.

Then there's Volunteer Stadium, which accommodates close to 5,000 spectators located behind the main playing field. The stadium was recently constructed in order to facilitate the prior addition of eight more teams to Little League, increasing the number of participating teams from eight to sixteen. There are numerous fields for practice, batting cages–even a basketball area and all of this in the shadow of the towering mountain range.

The moment that the Valley Sports team stepped from the plane at the Williamsport Airport on Wednesday, August 14th, the experience of a lifetime began. Team members were greeted by their two team hosts, more commonly referred to as "team uncles" or volunteers who usually live in the surrounding area and give of their time to a specific team during the entire visit. The combined years of experience of the thirty-two uncles in 2002 represent nearly 450 years of dedication, with novice "uncles" having just served two years, while others are in the 30-40-year bracket.

The team hosts, usually in three vans after loading up the team and their equipment, then drive to Little League Headquarters just across the river in South Williamsport. During the trip, the uncles sit with the manager and coaches, filling them in on the agenda for the first day.

Once arriving at Little League, the teams are in awe as they get their first look at Lamade and Volunteer Stadiums, the most reputed Little League fields in existence as they walk over to International Grove where they will spend much of their time when not practicing or participating in a game. The "Grove" is off-limits for the public or the media. There are four identical dormitories housing all sixteen teams—four per dorm.

The Asian team stayed directly above the team from Valley Sports. The rooms are simplistic, exceptionally clean and orderly, with a separate room for the team manager, an adjoining room for the coaches and then down the hall, the quarters for the team, complete with bunk beds and a wall-mounted television. Just off from the team rooms, there is a huge shower area that can be accessed by the team next door—one of the various ways in which Little League promotes teams not being totally segregated from each other.

International Grove is constantly maintained by Little League's landscaper and staff. The Grove is always pleasing with lustrous flowers and plants, not to mention the large trees dotting the grounds, presenting a summer camp atmosphere. There is a 10,000-square foot recreation facility, complete with kitchen and dining area that can accomodate up to 350 diners plus an expansive swimming pool.

Depending on when a team arrives, one of the very first orders of business is uniform fitting. Team uniforms are ready and waiting as the team arrives and each player with the assistance of their coaches is suited up. At the end of their stay in Williamsport, each player will get to keep his team jacket and hat, which he is also fitted for. Then, it's off to the administrative building for team photographs.

The administrative building is the hub of the wagon wheel of the Little League complex, which sits on sixty-six acres just off Rt. 15 at the bottom of the towering Bald Eagle Mountains. The "admin" building houses all of the offices and is open five days a week all year long.

To the left of Little League Headquarters sits the Peter J. McGovern Little

League Museum. Upon entering the museum, one finds himself standing on a large turf-covered Little League diamond. Three sides of the field are covered with a life-size wall-to-ceiling mural of fans. To the right of the field swings a flag from every participating country of Little League and a scoreboard indicating the last World Series score. There are two rooms to the right of the main room containing various kiosks depicting the past history of Little League and a theater.

On the bottom level, there is a room dedicated to safety with articles about how drugs can affect young players and the way in which improvements in Little League equipment has improved over the years. The next room contains glass cases, videos and information about how baseballs, bats and gloves are manufactured.

The next section is unique in itself as there are pitching and batting cages that you can enter, and after pitching or hitting, you can review yourself on screen. There is also an automated running area where you can time your speed on the base paths.

The final area of the lower floor has a Wall of Champions, cases containing autographed baseballs and varied Little League memorabilia donated by former major leaguers, many of whom had the opportunity to come to Williamsport and play.

Back on the main floor on the opposite side of the mock playing field, there is a gift store and adjoining rooms containing team photos dating back to the start of Little League, automated viewing areas with highlights of past games, and a rack of bats containing a team bat for every World Champion of the past with the names of each and every player. There is also a Hall of Excellence where honored people like George W. Bush, 43rd President of the

LITTLE **BIG** MEN

United States and Dan Quayle, a former U.S. senator and vice president who played Little League Baseball are honored.

The final section of the museum contains other awards that Little League is committed to, such as Parents of the Year Award, Little League Good Sport Award, Little League Volunteer of the Year Award, Mother of the Year Award, Graduate Award and the Challenger Division which, provides an opportunity for physically and mentally handicapped youths to participate in Little League. What many people don't know is that Little League is deeply involved in other activities besides that of the Little League World Series. The organization enrolls a number of other youth divisions: Tee Ball, Minor League, Junior, Senior and Big League Baseball, Girls' Little League Softball, Girls' Junior, Senior and Big League Softball, Boys' Softball and the Challenger Division.

One of the most interesting things about the entire complex is a small statue near Volunteer Stadium. It represents Carl Stotz standing next to a young Little League player. I often wonder if many of the teams who come to Williamsport really have the time to realize where they are and what they are a part of. What Carl Stotz started back in 1938, has affected not only the youth of our nation, but youngsters around the world.

Valley Sports of Louisville, Kentucky, and fifteen other teams of players from around the world were about to begin yet another chapter in the fifty-six golden years of youngsters playing ball in this community in late August. On August 25th, when all thirty-two games had been played, who would be crowned the 56th Little League World Champion? What new records would be broken? Who would be the heros in 2002? These sixteen teams had come a long way just to get to Williamsport. The toughest part of the journey would soon begin.

THE PROMISED LAND

In my opinion, winning the Little League World Series ranks right up there with winning a gold medal at the Olympics. Few people get to participate in the Olympics, let alone carry home a gold medal. Rare teams get to come to Williamsport. Only one will walk away with the championship.

In a way, it's similar to running a marathon. Not many in life can or even desire to run 26 miles, 385 yards at one time. Years ago, I had the desire to put myself to the test of running a marathon. As a matter of fact, I attempted this exploit twice. It is the most physically demanding thing I've ever tried to accomplish in my life. The end results of my two attempts are great examples of why winning the Little League World Championship is similar.

When you participate in a marathon, you are eventually faced with something called "hitting the wall." It happened to me on both occasions around the nineteen-mile marker. Hitting the wall is a term that is used in running circles to describe the feeling that one gets when you have absolutely no strength left. You can no longer take a single step or raise your arms. It is the most devastating sensation of total exhaustion that one can imagine. The first time I hit the wall I wasn't mentally prepared and I had to drop out.

The second time I attempted to run the marathon the dreaded wall was still there, and just like I expected, I hit it at the same point. I had to really dig down deep to keep moving forward. The last seven miles of the race were more difficult than the first nineteen. Looking ahead and trying to imagine crossing the finish line seemed impossible. I had to break the remainder of the race down into smaller races. Looking up the road I'd say to myself, "Okay, just get to that old barn. It's only fifty yards away." Then just as I was about to pass the barn I set my next goal at a telephone pole a little farther up the road and on and on until I finally reached the finish line.

LITTLE **BIG** MEN

The team from Valley Sports had already raced the first nineteen miles as they won the Great Lakes Regionals. Now, it was time to dig down and discover what they were really made of. The last seven miles were represented by fifteen other teams with the same mission in mind: Going all the way! These young men had been playing ball and traveling now for close to six weeks, and the toughest obstacles that they would face during the journey were still ahead. Many a team had run this marathon in the past fifty-five years, but only one team would cross the finish line–a finish line that represented over five decades of players who have done some amazing things.

Valley Sports of Louisville had arrived at the epitome of Little League Baseball when they were named as one of the sixteen teams to travel to Williamsport. They were to become a part of ongoing history in this small community, on this famous field where many famous feet had trampled. A number of youngsters who played Little League ball in Williamsport have gone on to become professional athletes: Derek Bell who played for Belmont Heights in 1980, became a member of the New York Mets; Boog Powell pitched on the Lakeland, Florida team in 1954, and moved on to play for the Baltimore Orioles; Ed Vosburg pitched for the Tucson, Arizona team in 1973, eventually playing for the Florida Marlins; and Lloyd McClendon who in 1971 played for Gary, Indiana, hit five home runs and went on to become a member of the Pittsburgh Pirates. These are but a sample of the many youngsters who played in Williamsport and went on to the major leagues.

Professional baseball is not the only sport to benefit from the efforts of previous Little Leaguers at Williamsport. Jack Losch, back in 1947, played in the first Little League World Series on the Maynard Midgets of Williamsport and later on in his career was drafted by the Green Bay Packers. Turk Schonert, former NFL star played for the Garden Grove, California team in Williamsport in 1968, and Brian Sipe in 1961 was a member of the El Cajon,

California team and went on to be signed by the Cleveland Browns.

Over the years, many baseball Hall of Famers have visited the field at Williamsport. Heros like Ted Williams, Joe Dimaggio, Mickey Mantle, Stan Musial and Carlton Fisk, plus many other noted individuals of fame who grew up playing Little League Baseball like, Kareem Abdul-Jabbar, former NBA great; and well-known actors Tom Selleck and Kevin Cosner. The list continues on and on, including even famed sports commentators Howard Cosell, Jim McKay and Chris Schenkle.

Like most teams who visit Howard J. Lamade Field for the first time, it must be just a bit overwhelming. I'm sure the team from Valley Sports experienced this feeling when they first arrived. This is an event that many who play Little League watch each year on television and then to actually wind up getting to the Little League World Series must be an incredible sensation. The stadium must have appeared as enormous for this group of all-stars who came from a league of just six teams with seating for somewhere around two hundred. But it's only the packaging that's different—it's still all about Little League Baseball. Even though the playing field may present the impression of a major league facility, the basic dimensions are the same ones as these kids played with all year long.

I've really got to give credit to the coaching staff of Valley Sports. This team had been drilled on the basics since late June and had continued to do so. The rigid hours of practice had paid off and they had reached their goal of getting to Williamsport. This group of players had been coached as hard as any team that was at the tournament. The repetition of the standard fundamentals combined with the relentless support of the coaches and parents was the primary ingredient that had taken Valley Sports this far.

LITTLE BIG MEN

After the team got settled in, the coaches gave the team two different choices: Ease up and enjoy the great experience of being a part of the tournament or continue to practice hard and try to win. The team conducted a half-hour meeting and came up with the decision, "Let's go for it!"

The Valley Sports players had made the concession to "reach for the brass ring," as they say, but, win or lose, this was to be a glorious moment for each and every player. No matter what the outcome was to be at the close of the tournament, these kids would be taking a memory back home with them that would continue for a lifetime. At some point in the future, they would be able to tell, if not bring, their own children to Williamsport and show them where they had participated in the Little League World Series Playoffs.

The experience of Little League is not solely for the youngsters who travel to Williamsport, but the coaches, parents and fans, as well. It has become a yearly tradition during the two-week playoffs to swap pins and buttons as hats and shirts are covered with past memorabilia of previous Little League World Series games. It's a great opportunity for players, parents and fans to visit folks from across the country and around the world to learn and experience something from another culture.

And, let's not exclude all of the Valley Sports followers who were unable to travel to Williamsport with the team. Louisville, Kentucky was pulling together for these twelve players who would represent the Bluegrass State in the World Series Playoffs. It was every bit as exciting as Derby Week in Louisville–a week when a joyful atmosphere hangs over the entire community.

More signs were beginning to pop up, especially on Dixie Highway: ALL THE WAY VALLEY SPORTS; WE SUPPORT VALLEY and on and on.

THE PROMISED LAND

During the days leading up to the team's departure for Williamsport, the sports section of the local newspaper was filled with articles about the players, who for the most part, were unknown to the majority of people in the area.

One of the employees where I work showed up one afternoon wearing a Valley Sports tee shirt. I had to have one! When asking where he purchased the shirt, he told me that Shively Sporting Goods just up the street was selling them for $10.00 each and that half of the sale would be given to Valley Sports to help with the expense of the trip to Williamsport. He said that he had to wait in line and that they were running out. During lunch, I drove to the store only to find out that they had completely sold out. The man who waited on me said that they couldn't produce the shirts fast enough to meet the demand.

Before long, vendors up and down Dixie Highway were setting up tents in order to sell tee shirts. Normally around Louisville, it's not unusual to see passionate Kentucky Wildcat or Louisville Cardinal fans donning their preferred team colors of blue and white or red and black, but now it seemed every one was wearing Valley Sports green and yellow tee shirts.

Selling tee shirts was not the only method that funds were being raised for the team. Valley Sports had started the year with approximately $30,000 in savings, all of which had been spent to support the team so far. It would cost thousands more, not only to get the team to Williamsport but to house and feed the parents.

Louisville wasn't about to let its team down. The Lt. Governor of Kentucky announced the team's request for donations to the media. Louisville Gas and Electric donated $10,000, a local bus company made a bus available to get the players' parents to Williamsport, and National City Bank threw in $12,000. A Jefferson County judge gave the team $500, Coca-Cola donated

LITTLE BIG MEN

$1,500, Fifth Third Bank gave $1,000, the Board of Alderman over $3,000, and the community of Middletown contributed $1,000, not to mention numerous donations from individuals.

Louisville, Kentucky was indeed proud of these young men, and by the many donations, lightened a lot of pressure from the coaches and parents, thus allowing the team to target in on just winning baseball games. The players were told to have fun—but underneath the thin veneer of hoopla there was a semblance of pressure as Valley Sports would be playing the toughest teams they had ever faced.

Despite the fact that there are teams from East, West, North and South from the United States and from other parts of the world, these youngsters share a common interest. They have journeyed to Williamsport to play the game of Little League Baseball—to play fairly—and win or lose—to do their very best. I wonder if Carl Stotz could have imagined back in 1938, when he began to put together a league for preteens, that it would have grown to such proportions of popularity.

For the Little Leaguers who make the journey to Williamsport, not only this town, but the great moments they will experience here truly represent the promised land. Valley Sports and the other teams in 2002 were about to begin the closing phase of the incredible journey.

LITTLE BIG MEN

And They're Off

LITTLE BIG MEN

The title of this chapter is more than likely the first three words that the announcer will say at the beginning of the Kentucky Derby held each year in Louisville on the first Saturday in May. The Kentucky Derby is one of the most, if not the foremost, horse race held in the world. The best jockeys and horses arrive in Louisville in May to compete for the most coveted title in horse racing—the first leg of the Triple Crown.

Only the elite travel to Louisville—and they come from around the country and from other locations on the globe. The best horses and jockeys will meet head to head to determine who will win this prestigious race as they take their positions at the starting gate.

The Little League World Series is similar as the best teams from around the world come to Williamsport to compete for the world title. These sixteen teams have survived weeks of tournament games as nearly 7,000 teams have been eliminated during the journey. Valley Sports is but one of the best teams in the world who will be stepping into the starting gates as the series begins. It will be a long contest beginning on August 16th and not ending until August 25th when during the championship game the superior team in Little League Baseball in 2002 will be crowned. Let's take a look at these sixteen surviving teams and see what Valley Sports was up against:

Great Lakes Region
Valley Sports Little League
Louisville, Kentucky 17-0

Southwest Region
Westside Little League
Fort Worth, Texas 22-4

New England Region
Jesse Burkett Little League
Worchester, Massachusetts 17-2

Midwest Region
Webb City Little League
Webb City, Missouri 14-0

Mid-Atlantic Region
Harlem Little League
New York, New York 14-2

Western Region
Aptos Little League
Aptos, California 15-2

Northwest Region
Waipahu Little League
Waipahu, Hawaii 11-2

Southeast Region
Southwest Forsyth Little League
Clemmons, North Carolina 13-0

Canadian Region
North Regina Little League
Regina, Saskatchewan 13-1

LITTLE BIG MEN

Mexican Region
Contry de Monterrey Little League
Monterrey, Mexico 24-7

Latin American Region
Los Leones Little League
Valencia, Venezuela 12-1

Pacific Region
Central Guam Little League
Agana, Guam 7-0

Transatlantic Region
Arabian American Little League
Dhahran, Saudi Arabia 5-0

Asian Region
Sendai Higashi Little League
Sendai, Japan 11-0

Caribbean Region
Pariba Little League
Willemstad, Caracao, Netherlands Antilles 7-1

European Region
Khovrino Little League
Moscow, Russia, 11-0

AND THEY'RE OFF

The 56th Little League World Series schedule was primed and ready to go as the sixteen participants were broken down into four pools. During the first five days of the playoffs, the pool play games would be concluded, each team having an opportunity to compete against the other three teams in their particular pool.

In the initial pool play rounds, a team can actually lose a game but still come back and play in the semifinal round and even go on to win the world series as the first pool play is double elimination. When pool play games have been finished, there are eight remaining teams who will vie for the world title—four United States teams and four International Teams. The first-place team in pool B will face the second-place team in pool A, while the first-place pool A team will battle the second-place finisher in pool B. The same line of play will be played in the other two remaining pools, as well.

On August 21st and 22nd, in single elimination format, the semifinals will be completed for the United States and International Teams. August 23rd is an open day—no games played. On the 24th, the United States Champion and the International Champion will be decided, which leads to the World Series Championship game played on Sunday, August 25th. Let's look at the four individual pools and the schedule for the pool play rounds:

Pool A	Pool B
Southwest	Mid-Atlantic
New England	Great Lakes
Midwest	West
Northwest	Southeast

LITTLE BIG MEN

Pool C	Pool D
Latin America	Asia
Canada	Caribbean
Pacific	Mexico
Transatlantic	Europe

Friday, August 16th

New England vs. Northwest

Transatlantic vs. Canada

Midwest vs. Southwest

Saturday, August 17th

Pacific vs. Latin America

West vs. Great Lakes

Mid-Atlantic vs. Southeast

Mexico vs. Caribbean

Europe vs. Asia

New England vs. Midwest

Sunday August, 18th

Southeast vs, West

Northwest vs. Southwest

Transatlantic vs. Pacific

Great Lakes vs. Mid-Atlantic

Mexico vs. Europe

Monday August, 19th

Europe vs. Caribbean

New England vs. Southwest

Asia vs. Mexico

AND THEY'RE OFF

Canada vs. Latin America
Midwest vs. Northwest

Tuesday August, 20th

Asia vs. Caribbean
Canada vs. Pacific
West vs. Mid-Atlantic
Transatlantic vs. Latin America
Southeast vs. Great Lakes

When it's all said and done, what team will be left standing from these sixteen ball clubs? Each one of these teams brings a great season history with them into the tournament. During the fifty-six years of Little League World Series Championships, how have these individual states and countries fared in Williamsport?

The Valley Sports Little League team of Louisville, Kentucky is only the third team from Kentucky to make an appearance in Williamsport, the two previous teams, both from Lexington, Kentucky, having traveled to Williamsport in 1971 and 1978. No Kentucky team has ever made it all the way to the championship game. The 2002 Kentucky team takes a tournament profile of 17-0 into the final step of the journey outscoring their opponents by a wide margin, allowing only one team to score more than a single run during any game and that was just four. In seventeen games, Valley Sports was involved in nine shutouts and seven games where they allowed only one run. Their pitching and defense can only be described as sublime and their scoring ability is audacious, especially during the district and state tournaments. In the regional games, their great pitching and defense continued but the amount of runs they scored had depreciated to no more than a high of five, which was far below their average game score except in the regional final when

LITTLE BIG MEN

they advanced to Williamsport beating the team from Indiana 8-1.

Westside Little League of Fort Worth, Texas, is the twelfth team from Texas to make an appearance in Williamsport. Teams from Texas have made it to the championship game on six occasions, winning once back in 1950, when a team from Houston took the title. Another team from Fort Worth played in the final game in 1960, but lost to a team from Levittown, Pennsylvania. Fort Worth's record before arriving in Williamsport is 22-4.

Jesse Burkett Little League of Worchester, Massachusetts is representing its state who has been to Williamsport six times in the past, but has never been to the championship final. Worchester's tournament results totaled 17-2, twelve of their victories shutouts.

Webb City Little League of Webb City, Missouri is the very first team hailing from the "Show Me State" to garner a trip to Williamsport. During tournament play games, the team went undefeated at 14-0, outscoring their rivals by an impressive 127-21.

Harlem Little League, representing the state of New York, becomes the fourteenth team to cross over the state line into Pennsylvania and come to Williamsport. New York ball teams have participated in three world series games and actually won the title in 1954 and 1964. The 1954 World Series Championship produced more major leaguers than any other series played: Jim Barbieri, Bill Conners, Carl Taylor, Boog Powell and Ken Hubbs. The Harlem squad brings a 14-2 record to Williamsport.

Aptos Little League of Aptos, California carries to Williamsport an outstanding state appearance, California having gone to Williamsport thirty-seven times. California has been in nineteen World Series games, winning the

World Series five times. The Aptos team walked into Williamsport sporting a win-lose record of 15-2.

The Southwest Forsyth Little League of Clemmons, North Carolina, like Kentucky, is only the third team from North Carolina to get to Williamsport, and on both previous occasions, they did not get to the championship game. They bring to the World Series Tournament a great record of 13-0.

Waipahu Little League of Waipahu, Hawaii has brought the state's total number of trips to Williamsport to seven, just one of those teams playing in the championship battle in 1988 when Pearl City, Hawaii, was defeated by a team from Tai-Chung Chinese Taipei. The Hawiian players earned their way to Williamsport with a record of 11-2.

Los Leones Little League of Valencia, Venezuela is the ninth team from this country that has made it to Williamsport. Teams from Venezuela have participated in two World Championship games and won them both in 1994 and 2000. Their 2002 tournament record stands at 12-1.

North Regina Little League of Regina, Saskatchewan, registers the 2002 journey as the forty-fourth Canadian Little League ball club to visit Williamsport, however, this is the first trip for a team from Saskatchewan. Canada has never made it to the final game of the World Series. They arrive in Williamsport boasting a 13-1 win record.

Central Guam Little League from Agana, Guam, is the first team from Guam to make an appearance in Williamsport. Undefeated at 7-0, they did not allow more than three runs in any one game.

Arabian American Little League of Dhahran, Saudi Arabia, embodies the twelfth time this country has come to Williamsport, but has yet to play in the World Series Championship game. They are undefeated in 2002 tournament play at 5-0.

Sendai Higashi Little League from Sendai, Japan, is the twelfth team from Japan to go to Williamsport. They have played in six championship title games, won top honors in five out of the six played and won back-to-back Little League World titles in 1967 and 1968. As a matter of fact, Japan is returning as the 2001 World Series Champion with a tournament record of 11-0, never allowing a total of more than two runs in a game.

Pariba Little League of Willemstad, Curacao, Netherlands Antilles, made only one other appearance in Williamsport and that occurred in 1980 when they did not reach the final game. During tournament play, they only lost one game bringing their game total to 7-1.

Contry de Monterrey Little League of Monterrey, Mexico, makes their country's sixteenth trip to the Little League World Series. In their fifteen previous appearances, they have played in five championship games of which they won three. The team from Mexico made their way to Williamsport with a record of 24-7.

Khovrino Little League of Moscow, Russia, is making their debut for the first time in Williamsport. Their victory record of 11-0 made them one of seven teams who came to Williamsport as undefeated.

The best Little League teams in the world had assembled in Williamsport. The tournament was about to get under way. Soon they would be at the starting gates; the race for the title of World Champion would be at hand. Just like the horses at the Kentucky Derby, all sixteen teams would have an equal shot at winning the race. The Kentucky Derby has produced some great champions with unusual names like Secretariat, Man-o-War, and Spend A Buck. On August 25th, when the final out is recorded, one team in Williamsport will walk away with the much-deserved status of Little League World Champions.

The twelve players from Kentucky (Louisville's Boys of Summer) with their unusual nicknames: Peanut, Oz, Jrob, Elk, Mad Dog, Big A, EEEE, Max, Pudge, CJ, Waldo, and Jynx awaited their first outing in the 2002 Little League World Series Playoffs. Back in June when reaching Williamsport seemed a long distance off and to most teams one of impossibility, it now was reality for Valley Sports of Louisville. These twelve boys would have to play the best games of their lives if they expected to survive.

—LITTLE—
BIG
—MEN—

Five Stones and a Sling

FIVE STONES AND A SLING

One of the most popular and well-read stories in the Bible is that of David and Goliath. David, a simplistic shepherd with no more than five round, smooth stones and a sling, faces the giant Goliath, a callous warrior standing close to ten-feet in height. The final result of the story is that David defeats the mighty giant, despite the fact that the odds against him seemed overwhelming. It's the ultimate story of the thought-to-be-weak triumphing over the strong–little winning out over what seems immense.

Each one of the sixteen teams that were poised to offer up their very best abilities in Williamsport could all be described as giants. After all, these teams did not make it this far by means of pure luck, but they had earned the right to be a part of the World Series Playoffs. These teams had defeated the best contenders in their cities, districts, states and regions and in the case of international teams–their country. These were the best that Little League Baseball had to offer.

These teams represented a higher level of playing ball than just the average team, but even so, when you weigh everything out in talking about the best of the best, there are giants among giants. What I mean is that there are always teams each year that reach Williamsport that are more publicized or that seem to have an edge even before the competition begins. There are "David teams" and "Goliath teams."

If there was a dark horse that would tip the apple cart in 2002, who was it to be? Coming into the tournament I really don't think the Valley Sports team was thought of as a powerhouse, nor do I think they were looked upon as a pushover. They probably rated somewhere in the middle of the competition. As far as super star status was concerned, Kentucky could really only boast of two players, which is not unusual for most teams. It is indeed rare that a team has more than one or two superstars. In Kentucky's situation, we have Aaron Alvey and Zack Osbourne who could both pitch and hit. This is to take nothing away from the other ten players as the firm defense of the entire Valley Sports team labeled them as tough to score on. They had outscored their opponents in seventeen games by a margin of 110-11, only allowing one team to score more than one run in a game. Kentucky would have to wait for their debut in the Little League Playoffs as they were not scheduled to play on opening day.

On Thursday, August 15th, Little League sponsored a picnic held in International Grove for teams and family members only. More than likely this is the first chance, with Valley Sports flying in and their parents coming by way of bus, that they have had a moment to meet and talk. It opens the door for teams to meet other players, from not only other regions of the United States but from around the world. Parents can also share with parents of other teams the experience of following their kids through the various levels of tournament play.

Later in the afternoon following a morning practice on Friday, August 16th, Valley Sports participated in the opening day ceremonies as the team proudly paraded across Lamade Field along with all of the other teams displaying their regional championship banner. The twelve kids from Kentucky then joined their parents in the bleachers to watch the first three games on tap. For now they could only sit and watch as they got a visual sampling of playing ball in Williamsport. They couldn't get down to business until the following day when they were to take the field against the team from the West Region. This was not to be a day of relaxation for the Valley Sports' coaching staff who were also sitting in the stands watching and analyzing each and every player as they wrote down brief notes on hitting and pitching.

Before the opening ceremonies, about mid morning there is a short parents' briefing of which the news media is permitted to attend. One of the main subjects that is discussed is sportsmanship. By this time, there has also been a coaches' meeting and a pitching review where the umpires, of which there are sixteen from around the world, observe all players from every team that will or could be called upon to pitch to ensure that there is nothing about their individual style of pitching that would infringe on Little League rules and regulations.

The first game of the series playoffs was slated to get underway at 4:00 p.m. in Volunteer Stadium. Spectators and parents from both Worchester, Massachusetts, and Waipahu, Hawaii, sat with locals as they awaited the first pitch. ESPN2 was set to televise the initial kickoff game of the series. The last time that Hawaii had made an appearance in Williamsport had been back in 1988, when they had lost in the World Series Championship game to a Chinese-Taipei team 10-0. Massachusetts' last visit had been in 1994 when a team from Middleboro was eliminated from getting to the championship game. Following three innings of scoreless ball, Waipahu broke the ice in the bottom of the fourth when their pitcher hit a home run over the center field fence. Then the team added on a second run on an RBI single. At the end of four innings, Hawaii was on top 2-0.

In the top of the fifth, Worchester doubled home their first run then followed with a single, scoring another run while tying the game at 2-2 . In the bottom of the sixth, the game still tied, a Waipahu batter bounced a well-hit ball off the top of the left center field wall to grab their first victory of the tournament at 3-2. The first game of the 2002 Little League World Series Tournament was in the record books.

The second game of the day was an International Event played in Lamade Stadium an hour-and-a-half after Worchester and Waipahu played. The

LITTLE BIG MEN

Transatlantic Region team from Dhahran, Saudi Arabia, was to meet the Canadian Champion from Saskatchewan. Saudi Arabia had also played in a game on opening day in 2001 only to go down in defeat to a team from Tokyo who would eventually go on to seize the World Series. The Canadians from Regina were looking to end a long, dry spell of not making it to the final championship match, which goes way back to 1965 when they were beaten in the World Series game by a team from Windsor Locks, Connecticut.

As the game moved along toward the bottom of the third inning, neither team had scored, but then an RBI single placed Dhahran in the driver's seat by a slim margin of 1-0. Canada came right back in the fourth tying the game at 1-1 on a center field home run. Saudi Arabia was not to be silenced in their turn at bat during the same inning as a single hit combined with two wild pitches and a passed ball enabled Dhahran to take the lead once again, 2-1. Both teams were quiet in the fifth. Regina tied the game at 2-2 in the sixth as they loaded up the bases with no outs. A line drive that was caught by Dhahran's shortstop created a double play, but the tying run crossed the plate. The official game of six innings had ended and the first extra inning game of the 2002 Series was about to take place.

Canada was unable to score in their half of the seventh, but Saudi Arabia, after getting their lead-off batter to first with a walk, scored the winning run due to two wild pitches and a passed ball giving them their first victory of the series, 3-2. The first international game of 2002 had been logged.

The final game of the day and the second United States battle in Volunteer Stadium got under way at 7 p.m. as the team from Webb City, Missouri, and Fort Worth, Texas, readied themselves. In Little League's fifty-six years of history, this was the first time that a team from Missouri had advanced to Williamsport. The previous team from Texas to appear in

FIVE STONES AND A SLING

Williamsport had been in the championship game in 2000 when they had been defeated by a team from Venezuela.

The pitchers from both teams overpowered the hitters and after five innings, the score was as it had started 0-0. In the top of the sixth, Texas hit a double and a single scoring the only run of the game. Final score: Southwest Region 1, Midwest Region 0. The first day's work was over and the end results were as follows:

Team	W	L
Southwest	1	0
Northwest	1	0
Transatlantic	1	0
New England	0	1
Midwest	0	1
Canada	0	1

The statistics for the first three games played indicate that, of the three main skills required to win ballgames, pitching, hitting and defense–pitching had been the word of the day. Of the six teams that played, they had only managed to create a total of eleven runs on twenty-four hits, which averages out to four runs and eight hits per game meaning that no one had really come out with their bats blazing. The defense of the teams hadn't been that bad–only four errors had been committed. Actually, the defense of the teams hadn't really been tested as all six teams with a combination of approximately 132 trips to the plate, had gone down swinging fifty-four times. Great pitching had kept the score of all three games modest, but mistakes made from the mound had accounted for many runs scored due to wild pitches and passed balls.

LITTLE **BIG** MEN

Three teams had taken their first game and were now only five games away from winning the World Series. Three teams had lost their initial game and were one game closer to elimination. The coaches and players from the winning and losing teams would turn in for the night with thoughts of the past day's events still fresh in their minds. Those who had come out on top would be elated as they had their first victory beneath their belts and were looking ahead to their next contest. Those who had swallowed a loss would be asking themselves: "What could we have done better? How can we improve?"

Getting back to the "David teams" and the "Goliath teams" that I discussed earlier in this chapter. Of the three games played on opening day, no one really walked away being viewed as a powerhouse or even as a "giant killer." Not one team had completely crushed their opponent. No one had established themselves as the team to beat. It was still very early in the tournament and over the next few days anything could happen. The pool play rounds are based on possible double elimination. No one had been ruled out yet.

The first day of the Little League World Series Playoffs was winding down. The scheduled games for the day had ended, but the day was far from over. Work crews were busy preparing the field in both stadiums for the next day's matchups. Workers were sweeping and cleaning the stands where countless paper containers, discarded napkins and strewn popcorn were seemingly everywhere. Food vendors were closing their booths, taking inventory for the next day's needs or just sitting around taking a much-deserved breather. Photographers and sports reporters were busy sending their individual headlines to their papers back home, while the local newspaper was preparing the news for the following day's sports news.

FIVE STONES AND A SLING

I have taken walks down by the stadium in the evening after the games for that day have long since been played. It's not uncommon to spot parents out for an evening stroll down by the practice fields or spending quality times with the players. When I say quality time—that's exactly what I mean as parents are only permitted an hour or so daily with their child and the dormitories are off limits to the parents.

The parents have journeyed just as far as the kids when they get to Williamsport. Most of the parents of Valley Sports traveled together on a chartered bus from Louisville. They had sat through the local tournament in Louisville, ventured to both Winchester, Kentucky, and Indianapolis, Indiana, for the districts, states and eventually regionals and had worried about each and every game as the coaches and players had done. Just as the team had bonded over the past couple of months, the parents had also grown close. The camaraderie of the parents was evident and when they arrived in Williamsport they had to share rooms but there was no complaining. One of the mothers stated, "It's been a wild ride—an emotional roller coaster."

I have no doubt that many of the parents of the Kentucky players attended some or maybe even all of the games on opening day. They, too, would turn in for the evening wondering how their boys would do when they stepped onto the field the following day. Kentucky wasn't going to be starting off playing a "David team." On Saturday, at noon, they would be facing the team from Aptos, California.

California teams are always considered strong, as teams from the west coast get to play all year long. California teams have done well over the years in Williamsport. Aside from the parents and numerous fans that were to attend Kentucky's first game, I'm quite sure that the average fan may have considered Aptos as the favorite—a team that could very well go all the way.

LITTLE BIG MEN

The last time that Valley Sports had actually been in competition had been more than a week past when they had defeated Brownsburg for the Great Lakes Regional Championship. They had gotten in quite a bit of practice, but would the week-long layoff from actually playing a game affect them in any way? Would their pitching be sharp? Would the defense, which they practiced so hard, be up to par? Would their ability to outscore their opponents by a broad margin continue? When the last pitch was thrown and the final out recorded would Valley Sports stand as a team that had defeated one of the many giants of the 2002 World Series Little League Tournament or be a loss closer to elimination?

—LITTLE—
BIG
—MEN—

High Noon

LITTLE BIG MEN

For those of you who can remember the famous western film "High Noon"–it's the ultimate story of standing up against the odds and coming away the hero. Gary Cooper, the star of the film, is the sheriff in a sleepy-eyed peaceful town, which is notified that a gang of hard outlaws will be arriving in town at exactly twelve noon. Their mission is to murder the sheriff to settle an old score. No one in town, including the sheriff's spouse, supports Cooper, informing him that he should leave town until the whole matter just simply blows over. Cooper refuses to wilt under the pressure and stands alone after everyone leaves him to face the dilemma by himself. Prior to the noon hour, Cooper spends his time alone wondering what is to come and if he will survive.

Valley Sports of Louisville was faced with a comparable obstacle during the morning hours on Saturday, August 17th, as they awaited their turn on the ball diamond against a talented California team. Unlike Cooper, who had no support, the players of Kentucky had plenty of support from their coaches, parents, attending fans and many loyal people who were pulling for them back in Louisville. Despite all of the support, Valley Sports still had to stand on their own feet and answer the upcoming challenge. As the clock slowly ticked away the time noon would soon arrive and the gunfight on the field would begin. Only one team would walk away with the victory.

During those few hours what could the team have been thinking? The players had no doubt been informed by their coaches that the California team might just be their toughest competition yet. Sure, they were 17-0 and had, for the most part, dominated the teams they had faced, but that was all in the past. How strong was the team from Aptos? Would their pitching, hitting ability and defense be better than that of Valley Sports? Remember, these players are only eleven-and twelve-year-olds. What kind of pressure were these young men feeling prior to their first appearance at the Little League World

Series Tournament? At this point, it was all speculation. The reality of the game would not take place until noon.

The fans, players and coaching staff of Kentucky would have to wait as there was an earlier game on this Saturday morning that had to be decided first. That was game four of the tournament between the Pacific and Latin American Regions.

At 11 a.m. in Lamade Stadium, the first international battle of the day kicked off, with Venezuela and Guam preparing for their matchup. Venezuela took the World Series title back in 2000, and was now back looking for their third World Championship. This was Guam's first appearance and indeed one of those David vs. Goliath games. Venezuela had been here before and had experienced great success; this was new ground for the kids from the Central Guam Little League.

After Guam failed to score in the opening inning, the Los Leones Little League team of Latin America, at bat in the bottom of the first inning scored five runs and broke the game wide open. In the fourth inning, Guam managed to score one run, but it equaled no gain as Venezuela, in their half of the fourth tacked on another two runs by means of a home run hit by the team's short-stop increasing the lead to 7-1. In the fifth after Guam was unable to score, the Latin American team came storming back with another four runs, the final score 11-1. The team from Venezuela made it truly apparent to all participants that they were nothing less than serious about going to the top of the heap. They had completely overshadowed the team from Guam, allowing just one run on three hits. Unlike the previous day where the games had not only been low scoring, but decided by a single run, the first game on Saturday had been a rout and the team from Latin America stood tall as a powerful force to be reckoned with.

LITTLE BIG MEN

The moment was at hand. It was twelve noon at Volunteer Stadium and 4,400 spectators awaited the duel between California and Kentucky to fire up. ESPN2 had their cameras rolling. No less than one-hundred fans, including the parents of Valley Sports, had made the trip to Williamsport for the team's first game. During infield practice, as the coach hit grounders to the infielders, the team displayed a fielding exhibition, cleanly catching the ball and then burning exact throws to home plate and around the infield, all this to the cheering supporters of Valley Sports. Those who attended this first game came to realize that the team from Kentucky had been drilled at the talent of defense until it had become a way of life. They practiced like eighteen-year-olds.

Aaron Alvey took the rubber for Kentucky and started off by giving the Valley Sports' fans the shakes as he walked two batters followed by two wild pitches. A double by Aptos gave the kids from California a 1-0 lead after the top half of the first. The right-handed pitcher from Aptos continued to give the Great Lakes' fans nightmares as he struck out the first six Kentucky batters. Things seemed bleak for the team from Louisville. Nothing was working right.

In Kentucky's half of the third inning, the Valley Sports' fans finally got a break as their team came back scoring three runs. Following a Wes Jenkins double and a sacrifice bunt laid down by Alex Hornback, Zack Osbourne drove the ball beyond the center field fence, giving the team their first lead at 2-1. The next batter, Aaron Alvey clobbered the ball over the center field camera tower, increasing the lead to 3-1. In the fifth inning, Osbourne once again brought the crowd out of their seats as he hit his second home run of the afternoon, giving Valley Sports their first victory in Williamsport at 4-1. After a rough start, Alvey finished up by striking out eleven batters and giving up only three hits.

Following the game Coach Osbourne commented, "This was a big win for us. We were kind of down in the dugout when they scored that first run. Once we made our adjustments at the plate, we started to hit the ball." Pitcher Aaron Alvey stated that he had been nervous and that this was the best competition he had ever seen. He knew from the very first inning that it was going to be a tough game.

Dave Anderson, the Aptos coach stated, "We're not used to anyone bombin' 'em like that. It was just those two kids!" Later that night, the coach from Japan approached Coach Osbourne, and having watched the win over Aptos commented that they would be facing one another in the finals. At this point, Coach Osbourne was just hoping to get through pool play.

Following Valley Sports' victory another game was getting underway at Lamade Stadium where Harlem Little League was slated to go up against the team from Clemmons, North Carolina. Back in 1999, a team from Staten Island, New York, had made it to Williamsport, but had been eliminated prior to the final game of the series. North Carolina's last appearance had been in 1998 when a team from Greenville had also been eliminated before making it to the final contest.

Harlem was the most publicized team at the tournament in 2002, a team that had been accused and afterward cleared of utilizing players from outside their district. This was another David vs. Goliath contest—Harlem looking very dynamic. There were a lot of New York fans who had driven down to Williamsport, including the mayor of the Big Apple.

ESPN2 was once again televising the game as the affair got underway. The first inning came and went without much excitement. In the second inning, Harlem grabbed the early lead following a one out home run, giving the Mid-

LITTLE BIG MEN

Atlantic Region a 2-0 lead. The third inning equaled yet another well-hit shot over the outfield fence as Harlem increased the lead to 3-0. Things just kept getting worse for the Clemmons team as Harlem broke out with an additional four more runs in the fourth inning as Jeremy Lopez hammered a grand slam out of the park, his second home run of the day. The lead was now at 7-0. In the bottom of the fourth, Clemmons made a slight comeback scoring two runs, cutting Harlem's lead to five runs. In the sixth inning, Harlem got two more insurance runs by driving another home run over the fence, adding to their lead. Clemmons' final at bat yielded them one more run, but it was too little too late with Harlem walking off with the victory, 9-3.

As four o'clock rolled around and the fourth game of the day was about to start in Volunteer Stadium, teams from Mexico and the Caribbean were getting ready to lock horns. The team from the Pariba Little League in Curacao was back for the second year in a row. Mexico's previous appearance had been in 1998, when they were eliminated from getting to the World Series Finals.

Mexico got on the board in the first inning, but Curacao quickly tied the game in the second with a run of their own. The game remained tied at 1-1 until the fifth inning when the Caribbean team sent ten players up to the plate. A single, double, fielding and throwing mistakes combined with a wild pitch gave Curacao six runs, four that were unearned. As the fifth inning came to a close, Mexico was down by a score of 7-1 .

Curacao threw salt on the wound by collecting another three runs in the sixth on two home runs and an RBI single, ending the game with the final tally at 10-1, the third blowout of the day, the only game so far that had been remotely close was Kentucky's win over Aptos.

HIGH NOON

It was back to Lamade Stadium again where the Japanese team was about to tackle the team from Russia. The Russians had their work cut out for them since the Asian team was the defending champion of 2001. This was Russia's second appearance in Williamsport and no doubt the most obvious David vs. Goliath matchup thus far. No one was really counting the Russian team out as Russia has always held a reputation when it comes to sports for being very talented.

The team from Japan completely overpowered the Khovrino Little League team. The Asian pitcher, Yoshinori Satoh, tossed a no hitter and was just two walks away from pitching a perfect game, which would have only been the fourth in Little League World Series history. The team from Sendai scored in every inning except the second. A home run in the first with a man on gave them the early lead at 2-0. Katah, the same player who belted the ball out of the park in the first, banged another round-tripper in the third inning, giving his team a 3-0 lead. Japan scored another run in the fourth, two more in the fifth and the final run in the sixth to close the game out at 7-0, the third game during the day that could be considered one-sided.

The last game of the second day of pool play began at 8 p.m. at Volunteer Stadium with 7,200 fans in attendance. This game, unlike the previous four of the day was actually the first event where two teams from the previous day were to meet. The two teams were Worchester, Massachusetts, and Webb City, Missouri, who had been defeated on Friday in two very close ball games. Both teams entered the game with the same line of thinking. They had both already lost their initial game in pool play. A second loss could almost mean possible elimination from going all the way to the World Series.

Webb City got on board with a single and a follow-up double in the first inning to go ahead by a score of 1-0. Worchester fought right back in their

LITTLE BIG MEN

half of the first, tying the score at 1-1, a double scoring a man on base. The deadlock continued until the bottom of the fourth when an infield single hit by New England enabled a runner to score, giving Worchester a lead of 2-1. The sixth inning was scoreless and Worchester had prevailed to advance in pool play as the Midwest Region was getting close to being eliminated in the 2002 Little League World Series Tournament.

Following the first two days, nine games had been played, with one team close to elimination. Fans had been treated to a little bit of everything: great pitching, a lot of home runs, some blowouts, and a couple of nail biters thrown in. The chart below indicates the pool play results after Friday and Saturday games:

United States Teams

Pool A	W	L	Pool B	W	L
Southwest	1	0	Mid-Atlantic	1	0
Northwest	1	0	Great Lakes	1	0
New England	1	1	West	0	1
Midwest	0	2	Southeast	0	1

International Teams

Pool C	W	L	Pool D	W	L
Latin America	1	0	Asia	1	0
Transatlantic	1	0	Caribbean	1	0
Canada	0	1	Mexico	0	1
Pacific	0	1	Europe	0	1

The scoring statistics during the second day superceded those of the first day by a wide margin. The first day's games had only netted a total of eleven runs on twenty-four base hits, while the second day produced forty-seven runs on sixty-three hits. More games were played on the second day than on the first day, with an average of four runs on eight hits per game vs. the second day's statistics of an average of eight runs and ten hits per game.

The second day of pool play closed with a number of teams scrambling for Goliath status. When you stack up the overall performance of the different teams over the first two days, Valley Sports of Kentucky had not reached the category of a team that could be considered a giant. True, they had knocked off the team from the West Region, a team that was thought to be a giant. Valley Sports' next contest on Sunday would be another great test. Another Goliath team stood in their way. It was Harlem, the most talked about team in Williamsport thus far in the 2002 playoffs. Would the team from Louisville, Kentucky be able to sling another stone and defeat another Goliath–The Big Apple?

—LITTLE—
BIG
—MEN—

The Wizard of Oz

THE WIZARD OF OZ

Sunday, August 18th, the third consecutive day of pool play was about to begin. Five games were scheduled for the day, with Valley Sports playing in the fourth at 7 o'clock in Lamade Stadium, their first venture in the stadium where the World Series would eventually be decided. Zack Osbourne would be called upon to do the pitching for the Kentucky team against the powerful Harlem team.

On Saturday, Aaron Alvey had stated that the California team was the toughest competition he had ever faced. Zack Osbourne was about to experience the same feeling as the Mid-Atlantic team in their first outing, had sent out a proclamation by defeating Clemmons, North Carolina, by a score of 9-3 on eleven hits, four of which happened to be home runs, that they were a team not to be taken lightly. The players from New York could definitely pound the ball and they might just be the most efficient team that Valley Sports had to face since they had started tournament play nearly two months in the past.

The long road to the World Series Championship Game had just gotten a little steeper for the team from Valley Sports. Zack Osbourne would have to hurl one of the best games of his life as he faced the Harlem ball club. If statistics mean anything Kentucky would more than likely have to hit the ball stronger than when they had defeated the team from Aptos. The team's defense would no doubt be as forceful as usual, but the question remained: Could they produce enough runs to take out the kids from Harlem? The answer to this question was a ways off as there where three other games that had to be decided prior to the battle between the Mid-Atlantic and Great Lakes Regions.

At 1 p.m. Sunday afternoon in Volunteer Stadium, ESPN was on hand to televise all the action, as 6,150 fans armed with hot dogs, popcorn, sodas and ice cream sandwiches waited for the first pitch of the day. The West Region was about to take on the Southeast Region, both losing on Friday and Saturday to the Great Lakes and Mid-Atlantic Regions. The outcome of this game could mean possible elimination for either Aptos, California or Clemmons, North Carolina.

In the first inning Clemmons came out swinging, nailing the first two runs of the game. Two singles, a wild pitch and a passed ball accounted for the first run. The second score came after a ground ball hit toward the infield was relayed to home plate to cut down the runner from third base, but the catcher dropped the throw and the runner was called safe. Aptos scored a single run in their first at bat, cutting the early lead to 2-1, with Clemmons in command of the game at this point.

The second inning was uneventful. But then in the third, Clemmons scored two more runs giving them a 4-1 lead, which disappeared quickly in the bottom half of the third when California locked the game up at 4-4 following three badly needed runs. The game was at the halfway point and Aptos could at least breathe a little easier. They had been down but had bounced back. It was still anyone's game to win.

In the fourth inning, Clemmons took the wind out of Aptos' sails with back-to-back home runs as they scored four more runs, giving them another commanding lead at 8-4. Time was running out for Aptos as the bottom of the fourth rolled around. Dave Anderson, coach of the California team, asked his players this question, "If we scored four runs in the first three at bats, how many would we need in the next three innings to tie the score?" The team agreed that they obviously needed to get four more runs just to get back in the game.

THE WIZARD OF OZ

The Aptos squad, just two innings away from possible elimination, not only got their four runs, but scored a total of six arriving in the form of two home runs: a grand slam and another with one man on base. As the end of the fourth inning, Aptos was on top 10-8–a remarkable comeback. Clemmons was unable to score any runs in the fifth and sixth innings, but in the bottom of the fifth, Aptos added yet another run to finally win the game 11-8. Clemmons had all but been eliminated and the team from California had dodged a bullet and would now move on.

As the fans walked over to Lamade Stadium for the second game of the day, attendance had hiked up to 9,300 spectators. Texas and Hawaii came into the game at 1-0 in pool play, realizing that a victory would guarantee them a position in the elimination round. The loser would have to win their final pool play game to avoid elimination.

Fort Worth created a run in the first inning following two doubles, then in the second tacked on four more runs on a double and a single—the score at the end of two innings was 5-0, with Texas in the lead. The kids from Texas continued to smack the ball, adding two more runs in the fourth and one in the sixth, defeating Waipahu 8-0. The team from Hawaii was completely shut down by the pitching of Fort Worth, which allowed only one hit. In the two games that Texas played, they had been one-hitters. In their first game, they had only scored one run, but today things had turned out much differently. They had proven that they could hit and win, minus the long ball. Doubles and singles–small ball. Thirteen hits had won the day. Texas became the first team to go 2-0 in pool play.

In Volunteer Stadium, the first international game of the day was gearing up. The Transatlantic team from Saudi Arabia, who had defeated Canada in a close game on Friday, was going up against the Pacific Region from Guam,

LITTLE BIG MEN

who had gone down in a devastating loss by a score of 11-1 at the hands of Latin America. The team from Guam was running on the edge of the cliff–another defeat meant possible elimination. The Saudi Arabian team came out hard in the first, producing four runs via a player being hit by a pitch, a wild throw, an RBI single and the last run reaching home plate due to a fielding error followed by a single. In the top of the second inning, Guam cut the lead in half at 4 -2 with a home run. But then Saudi Arabia scored, gaining the two runs back bringing the score to 6-2.

The third and fourth innings were scoreless for both teams. In the fifth, a two-run wallop brought the team from Guam a little closer, the score now at 6-4. In the sixth, on the edge of elimination Guam scored five runs, finally taking the game 9-6, another marvelous comeback on this third day of pool play.

In Lamade Stadium, the attendance was picking up, with 12,000 fans anticipating the match between Valley Sports of Kentucky and the Harlem team from New York. It's hard to say who the favorite was in this game. More than likely, in the eyes of most of the spectators watching, except for the fans from Louisville, the Harlem team was favored based on the game they had won on Saturday by dominating the Clemmons team 9-3. The Kentucky team had defeated the team from California, a formidable opponent, but the question still stood–could Valley Sports generate enough hits to take out the powerful Harlem squad? It appeared that it was another David vs Goliath matchup, with Valley Sports looking like the underdog.

Louisville bolstered the confidence of their fans in the very first inning by picking up a run on a single by Osbourne, who reached second on a passed ball and then third by a sacrifice from Aaron Alvey. Ethan Henry stepped up to the plate and following a sharp ground ball that Harlem's second baseman bobbled, Osbourne crossed the plate for an early lead of 1-0.

Osbourne was once again involved in the third inning as he hit a triple with only one out. The next batter, Aaron Alvey, was hit by a pitch. Coach Osbourne called for the squeeze play. Ethan got his bat on the ball, but the bunt was fielded smoothly by Harlem's pitcher who threw the ball to home plate where the catcher bobbled the ball for a brief second. Zack Osbourne was able to knock the ball loose as he slid safely home creating their second run of the game.

Harlem had an opportunity to score in the third inning with base runners on first and third. Jeremy Lopez, who had two home runs in his first game, was at the plate. One wrong pitch by Osbourne and the game would quickly change to 3-2, with Harlem in the driver's seat. Osbourne remained calm combining two fast balls and a curve to close out the inning preserving their lead of 2-0.

Again in the sixth inning, Harlem had yet another chance to take out Kentucky. With the bases loaded and one out, Osbourne and the team from Louisville found themselves in a tight corner. Zack struck out the next batter for the second out. With all 12,000-plus fans on their feet, Osbourne tossed an off-speed pitch to the next batter for strike one. The Harlem batter got his bat on the next pitch, sending it into foul territory. Zack took a deep breath, thinking to himself, *Get the out, win the game.* The last pitch of the game nicked the outside corner for strike three. Valley Sports wins their second victory in pool play defeating the Harlem team by a final score of 2-0. Valley Sports became the second team with two victories in the tournament.

The box score didn't exactly appear correct when you consider that Harlem got six hits while Kentucky only managed to collect a mere two base hits. Kentucky just seemed to find a way to win. It became obvious to all of the other teams that the Valley Sports' team not only had a great pitcher in Aaron Alvey but another fine hurler in that of Zack Osbourne. But, the fact still remained—when would the Valley Sports team start to hit the ball? It almost seemed as if they were flirting with elimination by winning two close games. On the other hand, they were becoming a giant slayer as they had defeated both the teams from Aptos and Harlem.

The last game of the day was between two teams that had to win. Mexico had been beaten on Saturday by the Caribbean team 10-1 and the Russian team had been defeated by Japan, also on Saturday, with a score of 7-0. The results of this last game on Sunday would produce the third possible team that could be eliminated from the playoffs.

A single home run in the first inning gave Mexico the lead at 1-0. The Russian team came right back in the second, scoring three runs on three errors committed by the team from Mexico. At the end of the second inning, the score was 3-1, with Europe in the lead. In the bottom of the third, Mexico cut the score to just one run as they scored, bringing the tally to 3-2, Russia still holding a slight advantage at just one run.

In the fourth inning, Mexico banged back-to-back home runs to cap the victory defeating the Russian team by a score of 4-3. Russia was all but eliminated, and Mexico was scheduled to meet Japan on Monday.

At the end of the third day of pool play the standings were as follows:

United States Teams

Pool A	W	L	Pool B	W	L
Southwest	2	0	Great Lakes	2	0
New England	1	1	Mid-Atlantic	1	1
Northwest	1	1	West	1	1
Midwest	0	2	Southeast	0	2

International Teams

Pool C	W	L	Pool D	W	L
Latin America	1	0	Asia	1	0
Pacific	1	1	Caribbean	1	0
Transatlantic	1	1	Mexico	1	1
Canada	0	1	Europe	0	2

Back in Louisville the idea was rapidly growing, the news that a team from Kentucky was getting the job done in Williamsport, spreading not only across the city but throughout the state. Valley Sports tee shirts were becoming the hottest item in town. I returned once again to Shively Sporting Goods to purchase a shirt, but was informed again that they were out. The owner just happened to be in that day and he told me there had been a three-hour wait as eager Valley Sports fans had patiently stood in line to get one of the shirts. As a matter of fact, orders were pouring in from around the state and throughout the country as former Louisville residents wanted tee shirts.

Friends, fans and neighbors congregated at local sports bars all over the city to watch the games. One of the more popular spots in Louisville was BW3's on Dixie Highway, which not only offered a great menu but over twenty-five televisions, five of which were big screen in order to view the games.

LITTLE **BIG** MEN

During Kentucky's first game on Saturday, fans at BW3's were very optimistic about their team, which had an unflawed record of 17-0. This was the first time for a team from Louisville, Kentucky, to make the trip to Williamsport and everyone expected the team to continue their winning ways. During the Aptos contest, local fans cheered every pitch of the game as they watched their boys win 4-1.

On Sunday, BW3's and many other locations around town equipped with televisions were packed with fans as Valley Sports challenged the tough team from Harlem. Following Kentucky's 2-0 victory over the New York team, fans were excited, because the team, now at 19-0, was just one game away from the United States Championship Game.

During the game with Harlem, Zack Osbourne was most definitely the Wizard of Oz, striking out fourteen batters, and, even though he had given up six hits, he had contained the powerful Harlem team shutting them out each time that they had threatened. There was no doubt about it any longer. Kentucky was indeed the "Giant Slayer" and one of the favorite teams at the playoffs. The Wizard of Oz had led Valley Sports to victory over New York–it was more than just Zack. Troy Osbourne said it all when he stated, "We've got great pitching, good defense–we have a different champion every game." There seemed to be a kind of magic about this team. But was it really magic? Not really! It was all about faith. The mother of one of the players hit the nail right on the head when she spoke of Brian Davis, "I know he's our angel in the outfield, and the boys know the same thing. I think that's why the boys are fighting so hard.

—LITTLE— BIG —MEN—

Coming Up for Air

LITTLE BIG MEN

It has been said of life that whatever we choose to be committed to that we should remain focused, intense–always having our game face on. People who are successful at most anything will tell you that the above statement holds the truth. However, it's nice to take a breather at moments, to step back and review where we have been, what we have accomplished, after swimming the length of the pool under water to come up for a breather–to take a day off.

On Monday, August, 19th that's exactly what Valley Sports did—the team took the day off. This day off was by no means a choice the team had made–they were just not scheduled to play this day. It was to be a day of rest and relaxation. The players from Louisville were not completely off the hook. They had come to Williamsport to play baseball and on this day, despite the actuality that they would not be involved in a bona fide game, they would still get their normal two-hour practice in–just enough to allow them to keep their edge, to stay sharp.

Practice over, the team uncles arranged a parent-team dinner at one of the city's restaurants, an opportunity for the families to enjoy more than just a quick hot dog and soda together. Some of the boys went fishing in the Susquehanna River, while others paid a visit to a local racetrack. It must have been a great feeling knowing that they were undefeated to date and that they could relax for the day spending some spare time at the pool or sending off a short letter or postcard to friends back at school. Then there was the Little League Museum up the hill where they could literally spend hours taking in the history of which they were now becoming a part.

There were other teams off this day also, some heading off to an amusement park for the afternoon, and some making the trip over the river to the Original Little League Field where the first twelve championships were played. In the press box behind home plate, there is a museum depicting the early history of Little League. During a research trip to Williamsport while writing this book, I visited the Original Field where I had played in 1959. It was indeed a thrill to stand at third base where I had played forty-three years ago. The original clubhouse is still there on display and, the Morning League Field where I struggled to make one of the league teams is still in existence.

I smiled to myself as I thought about all the kids that I played Little League Baseball with back then, realizing that we were no different than kids today. Standing there on that old diamond, I came up for some air myself and, for a brief second, my job back in Louisville and all the worries and concerns that I drag around as an adult seemed to fade away. I was back home in Williamsport, the birthplace of Little League. On the other side of the river, the dream was still vibrant as five games of the 2002 World Series Tournament were about to get underway.

Of the sixteen teams in Williamsport, ten were about to get down to business. The first game started at 11:00 a.m. at Volunteer Stadium with an international contest between the Caribbean team and the squad from Europe. The Russian team had suffered defeat in their first two contests, while the Netherlands had won their first outing beating the team from Mexico 10-1.

The Curacao team wasted no time in establishing an early lead by scoring eight runs during the second inning on seven hits, after they had scored a single run in the first on a solo home run. Their huge lead of 9-0 was increased by another run in the third and then three more in the fourth when the game was finally called due to league rules. The end results: Caribbean 13—Europe 0. The European Region had lost for the third time at Williamsport at the hands of a great Caribbean team who had pitched a no-hitter against them.

LITTLE BIG MEN

The Russians were now 0-3 and the team from Curacao was 2-0. The Caribbean team was rapidly becoming one of the giants of the 2002 World Series as they had scored a total of twenty-three runs in just two games.

At 2 p.m. the second game of the day started as New England faced the team from Texas. The boys from Worchester realized that this was their last chance in the pool play rounds and that they needed a victory to become eligible to play in the semifinals. This would be no easy task as standing in their way was the team from Fort Worth who was 2-0–a team that had permitted only two hits in as many games–a team that so far had not been scored on. The Texans had displayed formidable pitching and great defense.

The first two innings were uneventful, with neither team getting a hit. But then in the bottom of the third, New England scored first, getting four runs, three of which were the result of a three-run homer that traveled an estimated 250 feet by the team's pitcher.

In the fourth inning, the team from Massachusetts secured the win by tacking another two runs to their lead with three base hits, bringing the score to 6-0. The Texas team managed to grab four hits during the game but couldn't push any runs over the plate, losing their first game in pool play, their record standing at 2-1.

Game 17 was next. The Asian team at 1-0 presented an impeccable first game exploit against Russia of not only a no-hitter, but seven runs scored. The team from Japan had to face off against Mexico, which had also defeated the team from Russia.

The team from Sendai immediately put the team from Mexico away, coming out in the first, smashing a grand slam home run giving the Asians an early advantage of 4-0. The second inning went no better for Monterrey as Sendai scored five more runs on two doubles, pushing the lead to 9-0. The third inning was yet another setback for the Mexican team. Japan manufactured another two runs giving them their second victory at Williamsport by a score of 11-0.

The Asian team had also hurled their second no-hitter of the series. They were quickly becoming the most overpowering team and their best pitcher hadn't even taken the mound yet. With this win, Sendai secured a spot in the upcoming International Semifinals.

The last game to be played at Volunteer Stadium on the day advertised the Canadian Region against the team from Latin America. In their first game, the team from Venezuela had defeated the Guam team soundly, a score of 11-1 and was hoping to take out Canada just as easily. Saskatchewan had lost their first game by a narrow margin of only one run to the Saudi Arabian team and was focused on getting back to their winning ways, which had catapulted them to Williamsport in the first place.

In the first inning, Canada put the first two runs on the scoreboard, but it was an edge that would not last long since in the bottom of the first, Valencia scored four runs on two bases-loaded walks and two errors. The second inning created an even larger hole for the Canadians to crawl out of as the Venezuelan team scored another five runs on a three-run homer, a double, three wild pitches and an RBI single to give them a commanding 9-2 advantage.

In the fifth inning, Canada made a faint comeback of a single run, but it was not nearly enough to overcome the previous deficit and the boys from up north were, by all practicality, eliminated from playing in the World Series. It had been a strange game. The team from Valencia only gained four hits, but scored nine times while the Canadians managed to collect six hits, but only produced three runs. Canada's pitching had completely fallen apart at the seams, walking eight batters and throwing three wild pitches.

The evening game at Lamade Stadium started at 8 p.m. with the team from the state of Hawaii slated to face the Webb City team from Missouri. Webb City had lost two low-scoring one-run games of 2-1 and 1-0, which is surprising when you consider that they were dominate on the way to Williamsport, out-scoring opponents 127-21. This team could hit the ball and score runs but they had been silenced by both pitchers from Texas and Worchester only getting five hits and scoring just one run. The team from Waipahu had beaten the powerful team from Worchester, but then turned around and went down to Texas 8-0. It was imperative that Hawaii get a win as elimination was just around the corner.

The first five innings were nothing short of an ol' fashioned pitcher's dual, with neither team giving up a run. Then in the top of the sixth, Missouri struck back with a lone run that scored following a passed ball. With the Webb City team holding onto a 1-0 lead, the Hawaii team came to the plate just three outs away from losing the game. But it was not to be as a two-run opposite field home run sealed the victory for Hawaii.

Following four days of pool play with only one day remaining, the standings were as follows:

United States Teams

Pool A	W	L	Pool B	W	L
Southwest	2	1	Mid-Atlantic	1	1
New England	2	1	Great Lakes	2	0
Midwest	0	3	West	1	1
Northwest	2	1	Southeast	0	2

International Teams

Pool C	W	L	Pool D	W	L
Latin America	2	0	Asia	2	0
Canada	0	2	Caribbean	2	0
Pacific	1	1	Mexico	1	2
Transatlantic	1	1	Europe	0	3

Nineteen games had been completed at Williamsport. Four teams remained undefeated at 2-0, three teams stood at 2-1, four teams were even at 1-1, one team was at 1-2, two teams were at 0-2, and the final two teams were at 0-3. Of the United States teams, Pool A appeared to be much stronger at this point with three teams clasping a 2-1 record and one team eliminated. However, four more teams from Pool B were yet to face off in the last day of pool play, with the Great Lakes team of Louisville, Kentucky, being the only undefeated team in their pool. The International Pool looked more powerful as they boasted three undefeated teams and of the four undefeated teams, Kentucky seemed to be the weakest. Let's take a look at the overall statistics of these four undefeated teams:

LITTLE BIG MEN

Team	At Bats	Runs	Hits	RBI's	Errors
Great Lakes	39	6	6	5	0
Asia	46	18	13	14	0
Caribbean	55	23	23	14	2
Latin America	44	20	13	13	3

Team Allowed	Runs Allowed	Hits	ERA	S.O.	B.B.
Great Lakes	1	9	0.50	25	5
Asia	0	0	0.00	19	4
Caribbean	1	1	0.00	19	5
Latin America	4	9	7.10	18	2

In the hitting department, Valley Sports comes in last place with the least quantity of runs, hits and RBI's produced, while all of the other three teams are in double figures in each category. They did much better in the defensive area creating no errors tied with Asia for first. In pitching, Kentucky only allowed one run on nine hits, their ERA coming in at second best. More than likely in the coming days, Valley Sports would have to face one of the three International Teams who averaged ten runs per game, compared to Kentucky's three per outing. The 19-0 Kentucky team was running with the big dogs, but they seemed to be the least of the giants. Could they continue to win with minimal hitting and great pitching? Sunday, the day the 2002 Little League World Series Championship was to be played, was just days off and the kids from Kentucky were still in the hunt.

—LITTLE— BIG —MEN—

The Sleeping Giant

LITTLE BIG MEN

Tuesday, August, 20th, the last round of pool play was just about to get started. The teams that would participate in the semifinal games would be finalized and play on Wednesday and Thursday, followed by the championship events on Saturday and, then finally, the 2002 Little League World Series on Sunday. Of the five teams scheduled on Tuesday, Valley Sports was to be the very last pool play game played.

Following a day off, Valley Sports held their usual practice session, but would have to wait until 7 p.m. to take the field for their third game at Williamsport. So far, in their first two games, they had knocked off two giants—that of Aptos, California, and the team of Harlem. In their first game, they had limited Aptos to just one run, a feat that no other team during tournament play had been able to pull off except for a team from San Carlos, California, earlier in tournament play who had defeated Aptos by a score of 2-0. In no other game during tournament play had they scored less than two runs—as a point of fact during their 15-2 pace to get to Williamsport, Aptos averaged a little over five runs per game.

What's even more incredible is that Kentucky had stymied the New York ball club, shutting them down with a score of 2-0. The Harlem team carried a 14-2 record to Williamsport, dropping only two games along the way, but in neither game had they been kept scoreless. In tournament games, they had averaged around eight runs per game.

Aptos and Harlem were definitely teams that could score but, they had run into the twin road blocks of Aaron Alvey and Zack Osbourne, two young Kentucky pitchers who had surpressed their ability to score runs. The team from Valley Sports knew before they even got to Williamsport that they would be facing the toughest pitching and hitting found in the world of Little League. What the Louisville team may or may not have realized is that *they* were an intricate component of the great pitching to be found in Williamsport. Two kids that could bring the ball to home plate in the mid-seventies was nothing to sneeze at.

Valley Sports' "Giant Status," at this point was limited to their pitching and defense as their hitting had been rather mediocre compared to the other teams that were winning ball games. This was still a lingering factor in the minds of most fans. What would happen to the team from Kentucky when they came up against a team that could really hit the ball? Many fans were waiting for Valley Sports to break out with a high-scoring victory to prove that they could indeed hit. The fact still remained that Kentucky was the only undefeated United States team. They had already faced two different teams that could hit and had handled their lineups easily. Their 19-0 record would be on the line later in the evening when they faced Clemmons, North Carolina.

The powerful Sendai Higashi team from Japan stepped center stage in the morning game at Lamade Stadium. Their opponents–the Pariba Little League team from Curacao, Netherlands Antilles who was by no means considered second to any team in the tournament as they had defeated Mexico 10-1 and the Russian team 13-0 for a dramatic total of twenty-three runs scored during their first two games. In comparison, the team from Japan had gained victories of 7-0 and 11-0 for a sum total of eighteen runs scored. This was to be a matchup of two giants.

Of the four matches that these two teams had played in, three had been no-hitters, with Japan holding a slight edge of throwing two of those games. Actually, it was too close to call. Even though Curacao had pitched one no-hitter, their other game was a one-hitter. When you take a look at the stats, something had to give in this game. Both teams had great pitching–and both teams could produce double digit runs.

In this all-important game, Japan didn't go with the pitcher that hurled their first no-hitter against the Russian team, but went with a third pitcher, who according to the Sendai coach, was every bit as good as the first two boys who had taken the mound. It looked like Valley Sports was not alone in the great pitching department.

In the very first inning, the team from Japan gave their starting pitcher the lead, scoring three runs on a single, two errors, a passed ball and a fielder's choice. During the third inning, Japan still, with the lead 3-0, plated two more runs lifting the score to 5-0, where it would remain until the game was completed. Japan was now standing tall with a 3-0 record. The only bright moment to this victory, as far as other teams were concerned, was that the Caribbean team had managed to get three hits. Someone had hit Japan's pitching, but still, no one had scored a single run on their trio of pitchers.

At 2 p.m. ESPN fired up the cameras for the 21th game of the series. Fifty-five hundred spectators rolled into Volunteer Stadium to witness a game between the Canadian team that had yet to win a game and the Pacific team that was split 1-1. Canada didn't waste any time, scoring three runs in the first inning and then another in the fourth. The Canadian ace pitched five great innings of ball, but then in the sixth inning with a 4-0 lead, Guam, who was on the verge of elimination, fell just two batters short of going through their lineup twice.

The flood gates opened, Guam scored twelve runs in the last inning, eight of the runs crossing the plate due to three home runs, one of which happened to be a grand slam. Going into the bottom half of the sixth, Canada came back with three runs, but it wasn't enough. Thus, the team from Guam had made a miraculous comeback, defeating the Canadians 12-7. Canada was now out of the playoffs with an 0-3 record. The Pacific Region would be moving on to the semifinals.

At 4 p.m. it was back to Lamade Stadium for yet another meeting of two giants–two giants that Valley Sports had already defeated. Aptos and Harlem, with identical records of 1-1, and the winner on to the semifinals, the losing team suffering almost certain elimination. Both teams realized the significance of this game, so the managers started their best pitchers. The stadium was buzzing with 12,300 fans as they awaited the first pitch.

Through the first three innings, it was a pitcher's duel, with both hurlers only allowing three total hits, and the score at the close of the third inning at 0-0. In the top of the fourth, Aptos finally got to Harlem's pitcher. With two runners on base, a double to center field scored the first two runs of the game giving Aptos the early lead.

But Harlem was not to be quiet, scoring three runs in their half of the inning. A solo home run followed later in the inning by a two-run blast that traveled over 240 feet gave the New York team a one run advantage. In the fifth, Aptos was unable to score, but they could not keep Harlem at bay as they scored twice on yet another one-bagger with a man on. The game ended with Harlem the winner by a score of 5-2. Aptos chances of going to the semifinals had been dashed by Harlem who was moving on.

One hour before Kentucky would take the field, the Transatlantic Region at 1-1, prepared to meet the challenge of the Latin American team who had beaten Guam 11-1 and Canada 9-3. The Saudi Arabian team opened up the game in the second inning with two runs on a fielder's choice and an RBI single, giving them a 2-0 lead.

LITTLE BIG MEN

Venezuela quickly erased the lead scoring two runs of their own in the bottom half of the inning on a single and a wild throw tying the game at 2-2. After holding the Dhahran team scoreless in the third, Valencia grabbed the lead with a single run by means of a home run, the score now at 3-2, and Latin America in command.

In the fourth, the American Arabian team clawed their way back tying the game at 3-3 on an RBI single. In the bottom of the fourth inning, Latin America was unable to score and the game was now locked up once again in a tie. Dhahran scored in the fifth with three runs due to a bases-loaded walk and a single giving the Saudi Arabian team a three-run margin as they went into the bottom of the fifth. Latin America manufactured two badly needed runs in their half of the fifth, pulling them within one run of the Valencia team. The score with just one inning remaining stood at 6-5, with Dhahran barely grasping a scant lead. The sixth inning was uneventful as far as scoring, the Transatlantic Region walked away with a one-run victory over Valencia, improving their record to 2-1. This set up a three-way tie in POOL C. According to official Little League rules, Latin America gains the top seed since they had allowed the least number of runs scored per innings played. The other team to play in the semifinals in this case was determined by head-on play by the other two teams. Since Guam defeated the Arabian American team by a score of 9-6, Guam advanced to the semis.

The last game of pool play was just about to begin with the team from Kentucky taking on Clemmons, North Carolina. Valley Sports, the only undefeated American team at this point was favored over the Southeast Region team who had already been defeated twice. The outcome of this battle would be insignificant as far as the semifinals were concerned since Kentucky had already claimed a spot in Wednesday's playoff.

THE SLEEPING GIANT

The insignificance of the game only went as far as many of the 11,900 fans were concerned. Even though Clemmons was counted out of the semifinals and did not qualify for the World Series, they were still a force to be reckoned with. Clemmons had a 13-0 record on the road to Williamsport, scoring an average of seven runs per game. Even though losing to Harlem 9-3 and Aptos 11-8 this was a team that could produce runs—unfortunately the two teams they had played had scored a total of twenty runs against them.

The game was not taken lightly by Valley Sports, despite the fact that it was not imperative that they win. The pressure was off the Kentucky team as they had already assumed the spot as the top seed in the United States semifinals. Once again, the stats didn't add up. Clemmons had scored eleven runs in two games and was 0-2, while Valley Sports had scored a mere six runs in their first two games and yet were 2-0. Sooner or later, Valley Sports' hitting was going to have to catch up with their pitching and defense.

If they did happen to lose this game, what would the results be? After all, this team was 19-0. This team had never experienced a loss. Each and every player on this team had at one time or another been on the losing end of a ball game, but this collection of all-stars had not tasted defeat since they were put together back in June. Who knew what the results would be if they were defeated by Clemmons? The game was being touted as a "fun game," the outcome would not change the opportunity for Valley Sports to continue on, but the Kentucky coaches told the team that they were going to go out on the field and perform just like they always did.

This team from Louisville didn't know how to lose. Actually, they had always found a way to win. Whoever they were to face in the semifinals, mentally it would be better to go in at 20-0 rather than 19-1. In the eyes of many fans, this may have been a game that was not considered very important, but in the minds of the Valley Sports' players, it was just as important as any other game they had played in.

Shane Logsdon started on the mound for Valley Sports and for the first two innings equaled the efforts of Clemmons' pitcher, with the score at the end of the second 0-0. In the third inning, Valley Sports took the lead with three runs all scored on two outs. Ethan Henry hit an RBI single to center, then Casey Jordan followed up with another single scoring Aaron Alvey and Jake Remines. In the bottom of the third with a three-run lead, Logsdon shut down the Clemmons team once again. But in the bottom of the fourth, he had to be pulled and Casey Jordan took over the pitching responsibilities as the North Carolina team came to life scoring two runs on a double that rolled all the way to the fence cutting Kentucky's lead to just one run.

In the fifth inning, Valley Sports pushed another run across the plate, Henry smacking his second single of the game and then scoring on a passed ball, giving Valley Sports a 4-2 advantage going into the bottom of the fifth. Josh Robinson pitched for Kentucky in the fifth and Alvey finished up on the mound in the sixth. Clemmons could not muster up any more runs and the last pool play game was complete, Valley Sports was now 3-0 at Williamsport. The only other team holding a similar record was Japan also at 3-0.

The first twenty-four games at Williamsport had been decided and pool play was finished. Following five days of exciting Little League Baseball the pool play results were in the record books:

United States Teams

Pool A	W	L	Pool B	W	L
New England	2	1	Great Lakes	3	0
Southwest	2	1	Mid-Atlantic	2	1
Northwest	2	1	West	1	2
Midwest	0	3	Southeast	0	3

International Teams

Pool C	W	L	Pool D	W	L
Latin America	2	1	Asia	3	0
Pacific	2	1	Caribbean	2	1
Transatlantic	2	1	Mexico	1	2
Canada	0	3	Europe	0	3

The previous week, sixteen teams had arrived in Williamsport, every group of young players and coaches with the concept in the front of their minds to "go all the way." Eight of those teams had been eliminated and eight others would continue on. At this juncture, there was nothing but giant teams left. Japan and Kentucky stood tall, both with records of 3-0, the other six remaining teams all at 2-1. It was anyone's series to win. Valley Sports had finally arrived at the giant class, but had accomplished this feat in a humble, quiet sort of manner. There was nothing fancy about this team—they were focused, and they meant business. They were the sleeping giant in the series. On Wednesday, they would come face to face with the great team out of Texas who had only dropped one game at the hands of New England. The semifinals were about to get under way. Could Valley Sports continue their run at Williamsport in the humble, quiet style that had captured the hearts of many a fan?

—LITTLE—
BIG
—MEN—

Halfway There

HALFWAY THERE

It has been said, "Failure is the halfway mark on the road to success." Valley Sports along with seven other remarkably talented Little League teams had arrived at the halfway mark on the journey to the Little League World Series. Each one of these teams had played three games and was now about to begin the semifinal round. Two of these teams, Kentucky and Japan, had yet to experience disaster during pool play, since both teams were undefeated. The other six teams all had gone down in defeat, losing one game and winning two. Despite the fact that they had failed to win all three of their games like Kentucky and Japan, they were still in contention for the World Series Title.

The teams from Louisville and Sendai couldn't afford the luxury of dropping a game, if you want to refer to it that way. They and the other six teams were now in the single elimination round—one bad pitch, a simple error, one mistake and it would be finished. Valley Sports was sitting on a record of 20-0 coming into the semifinals and to ponder the reality that they were only halfway to winning the Little League World Series is hard to fathom. The twenty games that they had logged in the win column were certainly admirable, but a single loss from here on out could send them back to Louisville.

When the semifinals kick in at Williamsport, the level of excitement automatically gets turned up a notch. There is a kind of electricity around the Little League complex. While spending a week in Williamsport conducting research for this book, I talked with many of Little League's employees. I came away from this experience realizing what a great group of people operate this year-round facility.

While touring the dormitories in the International Grove, I spoke with the head landscaper who told me that during Little League week, it's difficult not to have a smile on your face. "Even emptying the trash seems like fun!" The employees working at the on-site gift shop told me that when the semifinals start up it's nonstop craziness as fans from all over the country and different parts of the world press into the small store for tee shirts, postcards, hats, scorecards and on and on. The kitchen staff in the International Grove is at work each day preparing not only three meals a day, but occasional snacks for the teams.

Speaking of eating, it's hard to envision the number of hot dogs, nachos, drinks and bags of chips that are consumed during the playoffs. During the semifinal games, the amount of fans jumps dramatically, hence the demand for food. Little League is prepared for the deluge of hungry spectators with forty-eight order-and-pick-up windows and a large pavilion with a number of picnic tables where fans can relax and eat. The day that I toured the stadium and the concession area, it was a drizzling October morning. As I walked past the concession section, there wasn't a single scrap of paper to be found on the grounds.

Back in Louisville, the enjoyment of having a winning team in the Little League World Series continued to escalate as fans assembled at local sports pubs and restaurants to watch their Louisville team take on the team from Texas. Everywhere you looked in and around the city, fans were sporting Valley Sports tee shirts in support of the team. Up and down Dixie Highway, it seemed like every other business was behind the team as they proudly supported the team with numerous signs: VALLEY SPORTS–ALL THE WAY; GO VALLEY; VALLEY SPORTS 20-0 and on and on. Everywhere you looked or went someone was talking about the team from Louisville. It was hard to believe, but the team from Valley Sports was still in the race for the world title as Little League champions.

HALFWAY THERE

The remaining eight games that would close with the World Series Championship would all be played in Lamade Stadium. From here on out, every game would be nationally televised. At 4 p.m. on Wednesday, the first International semifinal got under way as Sendai, Japan took on the team from Guam. The pitcher from the Asian team was the same lad who had thrown a ten-strikeout no-hitter against the Russian team the previous Saturday. In their three prior games, Japan had allowed only three hits and not a single run scored. Guam, dropping one out of their last three games, had allowed twenty-one hits and twenty-four runs to be scored. The stats clearly indicated that Japan had a favored performance heading into the semifinals. In every category of the game they excelled. They could hit, pitch, score runs and had a super defense.

After Guam failed to score in the top half of the first, Asia got on board with a single run, the score reading 1-0, Japan with the early lead. In the second inning, Guam remained scoreless as did the Sendai team. In the third, Guam managed to get a bloop single but could not bring the runner across the plate.

The bottom of the third proved to be fatal for Guam as Japan got five runs on a bases-loaded triple and a two-run homer. The game was now becoming lopsided with Asia ahead 6-0. In the fourth inning, Guam was not able to score and then in the bottom of the inning, Japan grabbed their fourth victory with yet another four runs, the score now standing at 10-0. Little League's ten-run mercy rule went into effect and the game was called after just four innings. The team from Japan would next go up against the other remaining international team for the International Championship game on Saturday. The team from Sendai Higashi Little League was becoming the favorite to win the whole shooting match. In the four games that they played, they had not allowed a single run to be scored while running up a total score of thirty-three runs themselves. Things seemed to be looking good for the team from Asia.

The next event of the day was the first United States semifinal game between Kentucky and Texas. The team from Louisville was unbeaten in three games, while the Texans had taken two and lost one. Valley Sports had only managed to glean ten runs on thirteen hits, while Fort Worth gained nine runs on twenty-six hits. Thus far, Texas had out-hit the Kentucky team, doubling Valley Sports' hitting percentage, but had scored one less run meaning that Texas was leaving a lot of runners stranded on base.

Walker Kelly was called upon to pitch for Texas. He was a youngster who in their first game against Webb City, Missouri, had recorded a one-hitter allowing no runs. His mound opponent was Kentucky's Aaron Alvey, who in his first outing against Aptos, California, allowed one run on three hits. Coming into the game, the pitchers appeared to be equal in their abilities.

Like the previous matchup between Japan and Guam, the winner would advance and the loser faced elimination. Fort Worth appeared to be a better hitting team and was by no means considered the underdog. In their three previous games, they had permitted only six runs scored against them while Valley Sports had allowed just three runs.

The 15,000-plus enthusiastic fans were in for the game of their lives as Texas' Kelly and Kentucky's Alvey stood toe to toe for six no-hit, scoreless innings of Little League Baseball. It was a record-breaking performance, since never before in the history of the series in Williamsport had two pitchers in a six-inning game pitched no-hitters.

The game went into extra innings and in the seventh, Louisville's Ethan

Henry smacked a two-out double into the outfield ending Kelly's no-hitter. On a wild pitch, Henry advanced to third but was unable to score as Kelly ended the inning with a strikeout.

The seventh, eighth and ninth innings remained, as the first six, Kelly and Alvey dueling it out, player after player on both teams going down swinging. Kentucky managed to collect two more hits, a single by Ethan Henry, his second hit of the day, and an eighth inning single by Justin Elkins, neither hit producing a run. Both pitchers had to be pulled according to Little League regulations as a pitcher cannot surpass more than nine innings pitched in a game. Alvey had been extraordinary striking out nineteen batters on the Texas team. Kelly had been even more deadly, fanning twenty-one of the Kentucky hitters. The two pitchers had combined for a total of forty strikeouts. Alvey had pitched a no-hitter through nine innings, a Little League record, while Kelly had only been touched for three hits.

Valley Sports' coach stated that Alvey's fastball had a little less zip than normal, but he had kept the team from Texas off balance with off-speed pitches. Alvey delivered 129 pitches and Kelly hurled a total of 118. Alvey commented that Kelly was awesome.

In the tenth inning, Kentucky called on Zack Osbourne who gave up Fort Worth's first hit, a two-out single, which didn't result in a run being scored. At the end of ten innings, the score stood at 0-0. Coach Osbourne had to pull Zack prior to the eleventh inning since he would have become ineligible to pitch on Saturday providing they won the game. It was a hard decision to make—a gamble. If they were to win this game, Valley Sports' tremendous pitching had to endure, but with both Alvey and Osbourne off the mound, who would they go with?

LITTLE **BIG** MEN

In the top of the eleventh inning, Michael Valdez took the rubber for Texas. For the second time in the series, Osbourne and Alvey connected with back-to-back home runs giving Valley Sports a 2-0 lead heading into the bottom half of the eleventh inning.

Of the three remaining players booked as pitchers, Kentucky decided to go with Josh Robinson. It was a judgment that could easily backfire. Zack Osbourne, who had been nothing short of magnificent on the mound during the series, was pulled. Everything was now riding on Robinson's ability to hold the lead.

Things got dramatic as Texas connected with a late-inning single. Things got even more stirring as the decision was made to walk Kelly, Fort Worth's most dangerous hitter, putting the winning run at the plate. A passed ball and a wild throw by Ethan Henry allowed the runner from second to cross the plate with the score now at 2-1 and Valley Sports barely holding on. With the tying run standing on second base, Robinson dug down deep and struck out the final batter to end the marathon game at 2-1, Valley Sports the victor. They were now 4-0 at Williamsport and headed for the United States Championship Game.

It had been a game that neither team deserved to lose. It had lasted three hours and ten minutes, just one minute shy of the series record set in 1998 in a game between Toms River, New Jersey, and Jennison, Michigan. A phenomenal forty-nine players had struck out, a Little League record, the previous strikeout mark came back in 1971, in a game between Gary, Indiana, and Tainan City, Taiwan, when the total number of strikeouts recorded was thirty-four.

The first day of semifinal games had closed. Japan and Kentucky were now set to meet the winners of the second round of semifinals played on Thursday. Texas and Guam were now eliminated from participating in the championship game.

Games 27 and 28 were scheduled for Thursday, so Kentucky gained a much-deserved day off. As usual, they would go through the daily routine of an hour or so of practice, enjoy some time in the International Grove swimming pool, and then take in Thursday's semifinals.

The first game of the second International grouping matched Latin America against the Caribbean team. The Venezuelan team had a record of 2-1, their single defeat at the hands of the Saudi Arabian team in a close game of 6-5. In two games, the Latin Americans had scored a total of twenty-three runs, allowing only one run scored against them. The Curacao team entered the semifinals also with a record of 2-1, the energetic team of Japan having defeated them 4-1. The Caribbean team had collected a total of twenty runs, allowing only four scored against them. Both teams were capable of braking the game wide open with double-digit scoring.

After Latin America failed to score in the first inning, the team from the Pariba Little League jumped out to a lead of 2-0 by means of back-to-back bases loaded walks in the bottom half of the inning. In the second and third innings, the Venezuelan team struggled to get matters underway and, with the game nearly half over, they were still trailing 2-0. In the bottom of the third, the Caribbeans struck again with an additional run on a double followed by an error. At the end of three innings, the score stood at 3-0, with the team from Curacao in the lead.

The single run scored in the third was to be the last run of the game, the last three innings being uneventful. The Caribbean Region marched away with the game and would now have to face Japan on Saturday for the International Championship Final.

The closing game of the semifinals started at 7 p.m. at Lamade Stadium, with two United States' teams going head to head, both looking for one more victory, a victory that would get them to the United States Championship game against the team from Kentucky on Saturday. The much-publicized Harlem team would battle it out with the New England Region.

Both teams had tantamount records of 2-1. The team from New York beat Clemmons, North Carolina and Aptos, California. The solitary game they had lost had been to Valley Sports of Louisville, Kentucky. The team from New England had gotten off to a ragged start by loosing their first game at Williamsport to the team from Hawaii by a slim margin of 3-2. Their next two games they came storming back, beating Missouri and Texas.

The first two innings of the game earned neither team a run. But then in the third, the action picked up as the team from New York forced in two runs in their half of the inning. Following a single, the New York team pieced together three consecutive infield hits with two outs enabling the two runs to score. Worcester fought right back and not to be outdone, tied the game with two runs of their own. A walk, a single and an error set the stage for New England's best hitter, Frank Flynn. Flynn flied out but the runner from third scored followed by a passed ball that created the second run of the inning. At the end of two innings, the score stood at 2-2. No runs were scored in the fourth, however, Harlem threatened by loading the bases with two outs, but was unable to score the go-ahead run.

For the next three innings, New England's pitcher kept the Harlem team from scoring and as the bottom of the sixth inning rolled around with

Worchester coming to the plate, the game was still deadlocked.. If the New England team could score in their half of the last inning, they would be headed for the United States Championship Final. If not, the game would go into extra innings.

With one runner already on base, the Harlem coach decided to walk Flynn, Worchester's finest hitter. With runners on first and second, the next batter flied out and it looked as if the intentional walk of Flynn had paid off as a wise strategy. Up to the batter's box stepped Ryan Griffin and after fouling off a number of pitches, hit his first home run, *ever,* slamming the pitch over the outfield fence giving the New England Region the win with a three-run homer and a final score of 5-2. New England was the first team in history from Massachusetts to play in the United States Championship Game.

The Valley Sports team, who had watched the game from the stands, now knew who their opponent was to be on Saturday. The dream that begun back in late June was becoming a reality. Just two more wins and Valley Sports could be crowned the World Champions. They had already won twenty-one games–two more seemed easy enough. Not so! First, they had to take out New England before facing whoever won the international title. Both games would be the toughest they had ever faced.

—LITTLE—
BIG
—MEN—

We Are The Champions

WE ARE THE CHAMPIONS

According to *Webster's New World Dictionary,* one of the many definitions of the word champion is "a winner of first place or first prize in a competition—winning or competent of winning first place; excelling above all others." On Saturday, August 24th when it was all said and done, two teams would be able to say that they were champions. One team each from the international and United States regions would stand supreme over the other seven competitors they had faced. Twelve regions had been eliminated from playing in the Little League World Series in Williamsport. Sixteen teams had been whittled down to four select groups of players who were now to vie for the right to play in the final game on Sunday to determine the world champions.

Of the twelve teams that had been knocked out of the competition, not one was considered a loser. These young men were the best that Little League had to offer. Even those teams that had lost every game they had played in Williamsport could go back home with their heads held high. After all, they had made it all the way to the Little League playoffs, a feat few teams ever experience. To their fans and their parents, they were champions in every sense of the word. It was an experience they would never forget, a moment in their young lives unlike they could ever have imagined. It had been a dream come true for these teams to make the trip to Williamsport to compete for the world title.

For four teams, the dream was still alive. One more victory would label them as either the International or United States Champion, one game from the World Series. The contestants had clawed their way to the top defeating teams in district, state, regional and, eventually, World Series playoffs to earn their spot in Little League history.

The first scheduled game on tap was between the Asian Region and the

LITTLE BIG MEN

Caribbean Region. The winner would walk away with the prestigious title of International Champion. This was to be the second meeting of these two teams. The first time they met Japan, shutting the team from Curacao down with a score of 5-0. In that game, Japan had only allowed three hits, their pitching had been golden. Twenty-five thousand fans eagerly awaited this return matchup at Lamade Stadium. Could the strong team from Sendai be defeated? Would the Pariba Little League team be able to bounce back and move on to the World Series final?

Japan lived up to the reputation of a performance that was nothing less than formidable. After keeping the Caribbean team from scoring in the first inning, they exploded with four runs, giving them a commanding lead early in the game. In the second inning, the Curacao team accomplished something that no other team had been able to do in facing the Sendai Higashi players—they scored a run! An infield hit and a double brought a run across the plate cutting the lead to 4-1. The fans were becoming even more excited. Someone had scored against the team from Sendai. The Caribbeans were going to give the Asians all they could handle. The excitement was short-lived. The game ended five innings later, the score still at 4 -1, and Japan still on top. Both pitchers had knuckled down, neither team threatening to score again. Japan was the 2002 International Champion and just one game away from its second straight title since a team from Tokyo had won the 2001 series. The high standards of the team from Japan became evident after the game when their manager stated, "Giving up that run was a bit of a shock to us." Whoever was to become the United States Champion would be challenging a group of players that expected nothing less than perfection from every one of its team members.

The United States Championship game started at 7 p.m, with Valley Sports of Louisville, Kentucky, taking on the team from Worchester,

Massachusetts. Even though the Great Lakes Region team was undefeated at 4-0 since arriving in Williamsport, they were still considered underdogs against the New England Region whose record was 3-1 in the series playoff.

The general feeling, seeing as how Louisville entered this fifth game with a batting average of only .192, was that they would struggle to score runs against Worchester. To date, in pool play rounds and the semifinals, Valley Sports had only netted ten runs while allowing four scored against them, while Worchester had pushed fifteen runs across the plate, allowing six runs by opponents. It seemed that Kentucky was still playing the role of David, while each team they had faced, except for Clemmons, North Carolina, was viewed as a giant.

The rumor was that Valley Sports could not hit. The manager from the Harlem team who had been defeated by Valley Sports and Worchester said, "Kentucky...they don't hit! I see Massachusetts taking it from them. I saw us taking it from them if we had gotten there."

The stats revealed that their poor run-scoring and hitting ability was more than just a rumor. Kentucky had only managed ten runs on twenty hits in their four games played at Williamsport. These statistics average out to a little under three runs and five hits per game–hardly what one would refer to as a championship performance. As a team, it got down to Osbourne, who claimed seven of the team's twenty hits. Alvey and Osbourne were the only team members to hit home runs and Ethan Henry was the only other player with more than one hit. The question remained: Can anyone else on the team hit?

Kentucky's manager, Troy Osbourne, laid the question to rest at a news conference prior to the game as he displayed a banner announcing Valley

LITTLE **BIG** MEN

Sports as the hitting champion from the previous day during an annual Little League skills competition. Kentucky could hit the ball, which they had already proven beyond any doubt through district, state and regional play, despite the fact that the "hitting switch" had been cut off after they arrived in Williamsport. They still remained the single United States team that was undefeated. The prediction that Kentucky's coaches had made way back in June that their strength would depend on their pitching and defense was now holding true.

The pitcher from Worchester, Frank Flynn, at 5'9" and weighing in at 206 pounds represented a large roadblock for Valley Sports. Flynn could deliver the ball in the mid-seventies. Prior to the game, Flynn said, "I think I can handle them. There's only two hitters I'm really worried about, and that's Zack Osbourne and Aaron Alvey."

Thirty-six thousand fans crammed Lamade Stadium to see if Valley Sports could defeat yet another giant. Zack Osbounre was to take the mound for Valley Sports. Could he wield his magic once again? Would they be able to hit Flynn? Would they finally break out of what seemed like a hitting slump?

The first inning was scoreless for both teams, but not without excitement. In Louisville's half of the inning with one out, Alvey was hit by a pitch. Ethan Henry then bounced the ball over second base, advancing Alvey. Jacob Remines at the plate banged a line drive toward Worchester's shortstop who snagged the ball and turned a quick double play, ending Valley Sports' threat. In the bottom of the first, Flynn clubbed a single off of Osbourne, but the young pitcher from Kentucky did not allow Worchester to score as he struck out two batters and got another to ground out. The score at the end of the first inning was 0-0, however, the scoreboard didn't tell the story that was unfolding. Kentucky had hit the ball hard and Worchester had gotten a hit off Osbourne.

The second inning was passive compared to the first, as Flynn got three Kentucky batters to strike out while Osbourne himself sent down two swinging. After two innings the score remained at 0-0. In the top of the third, Wesley Walden started off with a walk. Alex Hornback was awarded first base after a sacrifice bunt in which Worchester's catcher blocked Hornbacks' lane. Osbourne stepped up to the plate and he more than made up for the hit he had given up in the first inning to Flynn as he belted a single to center field scoring the first run of the game. Hornback then scored on a sacrifice fly by Alvey, pushing their lead to 2-0. Ethan Henry put two more runs on the board on a home run just inside the right field foul line, giving Valley Sports a 4-0 margin. In the bottom of the third inning, Osbourne coughed up his second hit of the game but Worchester was unable to capitalize.

The fourth inning went by quickly with four of the six players stepping up to the plate and striking out. At the end of four innings, Kentucky was still holding strong at 4-0. The fifth saw yet another threat by Louisville. Osbourne hit a long single and wound up standing on third from an error. Alvey was then hit by a pitch for the second time in the game. The scoring threat was stopped when Ethan Henry hit the ball toward Worchester's pitcher. Henry was thrown out at first and Osbourne, trying to score from third, was cut down at home plate to end the inning. Worchester could not muster up much offense in their fifth and sixth innings. The final score was 4-0, and Valley Sports was now the 2002 United States Champion.

Zack Osbourne sealed his third victory during the tournament and boosted his scoreless streak to thirteen innings. The Kentucky pitcher was overwhelming, as usual, hurling seventy-three pitches and striking out eleven.

LITTLE BIG MEN

Worchester's manager said that it was probably the best pitched game of the series. Osbourne gave up two hits and only one walk, with Worchester never getting a runner past first base.

Valley Sports, once again in their usual fashion since appearing in Williamsport, had been victorious. They managed to win on just four runs on three hits, matching their best run-scoring effort, which was against Aptos in their first game.

Kentucky fans at Williamsport were excited over the victory, 150 of whom on Friday, the day prior to the United States Championship battle, traveled the eight-hour-plus trip to Little League via three chartered buses. Many news reporters, who from the very beginning were of the opinion that Valley Sports was a fan favorite, were right on the mark. Great Lakes tee shirts and hats at the gift shop were being gobbled up by fans, not only from Kentucky, but from all around the country. The players were surrounded by fans desiring pictures and autographs. A congratulatory call from the U.S.S. Louisville was patched through to Williamsport, but the team was not available at the time.

Back in Louisville, Kentucky, the excitement continued to grow. A huge billboard on one of the city's major highways read: GREATER LOUISVILLE INC. SALUTES VALLEY SPORTS. People all over town were saying that Valley Sports could go all the way–just one more game to go. More signs by the day were appearing throughout the city in support of the team. Tee shirts were being sold at every intersection up and down Dixie Highway. Everywhere you went someone was talking about Valley Sports.

Kentucky was no stranger to having teams that had aspired to become national champions. The Louisville Cardinals and the Kentucky Wildcats had achieved top honors in basketball in the past. This was a basketball state–fans expected their team to win it all. Now, a group of eleven-and twelve-year-olds had put the state of Kentucky on the map, as far as Little League Baseball was concerned.

The stage was set and the final curtain would be raised on Sunday when Kentucky went head-to-head with Japan for the 2002 Little League World Championship. These twelve boys from the southwest side of Louisville, Kentucky, had accomplished what seemed unbelievable. They had won twenty-two consecutive games on their climb to the top. They had accomplished it in a fashion that not only represented Kentucky well, but also that of the entire country. These kids were humble, courteous and well-mannered, but at the same time, meant business. Without a doubt, they were warriors–giant killers. They could now say, "We are the champions!"

—LITTLE—
BIG
—MEN—

The Shot Heard 'Round the World

THE SHOT HEARD 'ROUND THE WORLD

The day had finally arrived. August 25th, 2002. At the end of the day, one Little League team would be left standing as the elite in the world. One team out of the literally thousands that had stepped onto fields at the beginning of the season would now be able to claim world supremacy in Little League Baseball. One team comprised of kids between the ages of eleven and twelve and their coaches had prevailed on the road to Williamsport. The finish line was in sight–they were sprinting the final lap of the race against a competitor who had performed equally. Neck and neck, the last two teams would have to punch it in, dig down deep and more than likely have to play the prime game of their lives in order to become champions of the world.

At 6:30 p.m., the Valley Sports Little League team of Louisville, Kentucky, would face off against Sendai, Japan in the 2002 Little League World Series Championship Game. Two groups of players, from not only different cultures but from opposite corners of the world, would meet on the field of battle more commonly referred to as a baseball diamond, in a quiet river town wrapped in the shadows of the surrounding mountains to resolve who was the best at the game.

At the beginning of the season, if you would have asked the normal person on the street in Louisville where Sendai, Japan, was located his answer would probably be, "Never heard of the place." Likewise in Sendai, the normal person from Japan would react the same way if asked about Louisville, Kentucky. But that was before Louisville and Sendai had soared to worldwide attention in recent days. These two cities represented the two best teams that Little League Baseball had to present in 2002. I don't think they viewed each other as the enemy, but rather that of worthy opponents.

This can be no more evident than from the example set by players and coaches on both of these magnificent teams. Earlier, during the playoffs at

LITTLE **BIG** MEN

Williamsport, Coach Osbourne was approached by Coach Kazutomo Takahashi, who said, "It would be an honor to play you–you guys like us." Osbourne commented, "It's an honor for him to say that as disciplined as their program has been." Japanese teams have always come to Williamsport displaying the highest level of discipline. The Valley Sports team was without a doubt the hardest worked team at the tournament in 2002, with their coaches demanding tough discipline at every aspect of the game. These kids may have only been eleven-and twelve-years-old but when it came to the game, they were nothing less than professionals.

The level of respect went far beyond just that of the coaches. During the playoffs, Sendai resided directly above Valley Sports in International Grove. Each and every morning, the players would bump into one another saying, "Hello, how are you guys doing?" Of course, much of what was said was not understood when you consider the language barrier that the two teams faced, but then, a simplistic smile or a handshake seems to be the language of the world. Everyone understands a smile.

The spirit of excitement in and around the Little League complex was at its peak. The staff and members that make up the terrific team at Little League Headquarters were about to experience what they had worked all year long to obtain. The championship game would be every bit as exciting as any sporting event anywhere in the world. The attending crowd would reach 40,000-plus, not to mention the millions of fans watching the game on television.

But prior to the beginning of the World Series Championship Game, there was one other championship that had to be determined. At noon, the consolation game between New England and the Caribbean Region was to be played. The winner would walk away with the coveted title as the third best Little League team in the world. The team from Curacao dominated the game

THE SHOT HEARD 'ROUND THE WORLD

from the start, collecting four runs in the first inning, two in the second, two in the fourth and one in the fifth, winning the consolation game by a score of 9-1. New England's single run came in the top of the fifth. Too little, too late. The Caribbeans captured third place honors for the second year in a row. In 2001, they had been defeated by a team from the Bronx, New York, but was later awarded the game when the New York team was disqualified. Like all the other teams who had traveled to Williamsport, the Caribbean team would return to their country as champions in the eyes of their fans and parents.

There was a time break between the consolation game and the final event of the World Series, but the hustle and bustle in and around Lamade Stadium was filled with excitement. The museum and gift shops were packed with visitors. Those who desired to make a purchase had to stand in long lines. The concession stand operators were gearing up for the throng of thousands of hungry fans.

Fans waited in line at the official Little League post office, a blue and white shed in the shape of a giant mailbox complete with, red flag. Referred to as Little League Baseball Station, this tiny kiosk sandwiched in between Lamade and Volunteer Stadiums is an official post office where fans can send off packages and letters around the world. It's the only post office in the world where a person can get the official Little League stamp.

Back in Louisville, Kentucky, Little League Baseball had risen to a fever pitch. Fans all across the city and even throughout the state were rallying at neighborhood restaurants and pubs to watch the 2002 Little League World Series. At Conway Middle School, the school attended by three of the Valley Sports' players, the gym was prepared for hundreds of students and parents to view the championship game.

LITTLE BIG MEN

The Louisville players had become nothing less than heros at the schools they attended. Conway held bragging rights to Josh Robinson, Aaron Alvey and Wes Walden. Throughout the week, the school had given announcements as to the progress of the team. A giant banner was hung in the cafeteria for students to sign wishing the team luck.

At St. Paul School where Blaine Madden and Zack Osbourne attend, the principal had provided daily progress reports on how the team was doing at Williamsport. At Stuart Middle School where Jake Remines and Ethan Henry were students, the classrooms and hallways were buzzing with excitement, as were all the schools that the players attended.

As 6:30 began to close in on what was to be the decisive game at Williamsport, the realization of what was about to get underway crept into the minds of both teams. Valley Sports was being reported as the underdog, Sendai, a statistical winner. Even though both teams entered the last game with identical 5-0 records, the team from Japan had arrived with a much more powerful portfolio. In the five previous games that Japan had played, they had out-hit their opponents 30-8 and outscored teams by a devastating 37-1. Their pitching had been awesome, their aces throwing two no-hitters and three shutouts, striking out forty-four batters and only walking eight.

At the plate, it appeared that Sendai also had the advantage as Valley Sports had only scored sixteen runs on twenty-three hits and had allowed just four runs. In the defensive department, Japan over-powered Kentucky in every category. But it was Kentucky's pitching that most bothered the coach from Japan. The two hurlers from Kentucky could deliver the ball up in the mid-seventies, a degree of pitching that was unusual in Japan. On this day, Japan was only going to have to deal with one of the two young men, that being Aaron Alvey, Kentucky's 5' 9", 175 pound ace.

THE SHOT HEARD 'ROUND THE WORLD

This twenty-third consecutive game would be Valley Sports' hardest challenge to date, once again designated as the "David team." Sendai was capable of scoring a lot of runs, and quickly, while their pitching was virtually unhittable. The team from Japan had been in four of the past five championship games and had gained two of the prior three World Series titles in Williamsport and seemingly was in the driver's seat to take a third championship.

There wasn't any doubt that the team from Sendai would be the best team Valley Sports had ever faced. Everything they had been drilled on for months would have to be performed like clockwork if Valley Sports expected to win the championship. Yoosuke Katoh, who hadn't allowed a hit in his last ten innings pitched would take the mound for Japan. The game was about to begin, with fans eagerly awaiting the first pitch as "Dugout," Little League's mascot, mingled with the players and crowd.

Kentucky was the visiting team so they had first cracks with the bat. After Katoh retired Zack Osbourne, Louisville's lead-off hitter, Aaron Alvey stepped up to the plate. On the very first pitch, Alvey creamed a sixty-eight mile-an-hour fastball that sailed approximately 250 feet toward the center field fence. As Alvey rounded the base paths, Japan was shocked. This was the first time since they had arrived in Williamsport that they had trailed during a game. The fans, who for the most part were supporting the team from Kentucky, sensed a glimmer of hope and the game was just beginning.

The coach from Japan paid a visit to the mound following the massive home run in order to calm his young pitcher down. In the series so far, Sendai had intimidated their adversaries by scoring quickly, but the roles were now reversed. Valley Sports had done what most folks were saying could not be accomplished. They had not only managed a hit, but had scored a run. The

LITTLE **BIG** MEN

Japanese left-hander settled down following Alvey's home run and got the two final outs in the top half of the first, but critical damage had been inflicted by the team from Kentucky.

With a 1-0 margin, Alvey took the rubber ready to face the top of Japan's lineup in the bottom of the first inning. The fans seemed very optimistic, but the game was far from being in the bag. In the previous five games that Sendai played, they had scored a total of fourteen runs in the first inning, an average of just under three per game. Thirty-seven percent of their scoring had come in the first inning. Aaron Alvey was about to serve up his best pitching ability against a team that had never failed to score in the first inning at the 2002 World Series Tournament. Would Alvey be able to tip the scales and defy the statistics?

In front of 41,000 cheering fans, Alvey dismantled the "Japan-always-scores-in-the-first-inning-theory" as he struck out their first three batters. His pitches were blazing past the Japanese hitters at nearly seventy-eight miles an hour. After one inning, Valley Sports led Japan by a score of 1-0. Alvey had displayed to the world who was boss. At least, so far.

In the second inning, Katoh regained his composure as he prevented Kentucky from adding to their slim lead. Alvey was equally dominant out on the mound as Sendai, after two innings, had yet to score. In the second inning, Alvey broke the thirty-one-year-old strike-out record of thirty-six. At the close of the first two innings, the score remained 1-0, with Valley Sports still out in front.

Little did anyone know that first inning home run by Alvey was to be the single run scored in the entire game. Louisville managed to grab two more hits, but was unable to capitalize and score again. Alvey had his pitching arm iced down at the end of the fourth, and then returned to continue to puzzle the Sendai players. Sendai got three hits, stranded runners in the fourth and fifth innings, but only managed to place one base runner at third.

Valley Sports, in the top half of the sixth inning, was unable to gain an insurance run to augment their slight lead. Kentucky took the field in what they hoped would be the last inning, barely holding onto a 1-0 lead. Louisville was on the verge of pulling off what most folks said was impossible–defeating the team from Japan!

Aaron Alvey stood on the pitcher's mound as he was about to face the meat of Sendai's lineup. The first out came easily as Alvey blasted three strikes past the first batter. The 41,000 fans were on their feet chanting, "USA, USA," as Japan's second batter of the inning stepped into the batter's box. Alvey remained tough as ever as he got the hitter to ground out to third base for the second out.

Alvey startled the crowd as he walked Sendai's next batter, bringing Tatsuhiko Numakara, who represented the winning run up to the plate. Numakara was the team's best home run hitter and with just one swing of the bat, the championship game could very well be ended. What a fitting climax to the Little League World Series! An underdog team with just a one-run lead with two outs in the bottom of the sixth inning, and the best pitcher in the tournament facing the top home run hitter from Japan.

Alvey knew he had to pitch to Numakara and hope that the Valley Sports' defense could hold on. The pitch came and Numakara lined a shot toward the right field line. It looked like an extra base hit. Casey Jordan, Kentucky's first baseman, snagged the ball instantly, ending the threat, which, just a second earlier, looked like the ball would go into right field for extra bases. With

LITTLE BIG MEN

Sendai's speed, the runner on first could score, tying the game and placing the winning run on second, or possibly, third base. The crowd was stunned–the game was over! Jordan, who had only managed to collect one hit during the tournament at Williamsport, more than made up for his lack of hitting. Great defense, one of the two main skills the Valley Sports' coaches had preached all summer, was the key that had ended the game and allowed Louisville to become Little League World Champions.

Forty thousand fans exploded as Casey Jordan speared that ball. Later, when Jordan was interviewed, he stated, "I was excited. I just said to myself, 'make sure you've got the ball before you celebrate'." Valley Sports' players and coaches embraced on the diamond, then quickly turned their attention to their worthy opponents, Sendai, whose players had broken down in tears. Jordan, displaying compassion, said, "I'm really happy right now," as he fought back tears. "I'm also really sad because they had to lose. They're a great team." The Kentucky team, disciplined and humble as always, signaled the Japanese team to join them in a victory lap.

In a pregame pep lecture, Coach Osbourne told his players that if they wanted to win, they had to play like eighteen-year-olds and that this would probably be the last time that they would play together as a Little League team. They would be moving on, playing ball on larger fields as teenagers. This was the last time these boys, as a team, would ever play baseball together. They went out on top of the world and Alvey's home run was most definitely "the shot heard 'round the world."

LITTLE BIG MEN

Going Home

LITTLE BIG MEN

Home! Has a nice ring to it doesn't it? When I think of home, I visualize the house where I live and all of the things God has indeed blessed me with. What a great feeling it is that after a day of whatever it is that we do for a living, we pull up in our driveway, take a deep breath, and walk in our front door to be greeted by those we love, be it the husband, wife, kids or pets.

At fifty-eight years of age, home has a different meaning to me than when I was twelve years of age. Back then, it seems to me that where I lived on Memorial Avenue was much more than just a two-story structure where I ate meals and slept at night. It was a secure haven where I knew my parents were always available to answer all the questions I had about growing up–where at night when I laid my head down to rest, there really never seemed to be any great pressure about paying bills or what I planned to do at work the following day. No, my parents probably laid in bed and worried about those matters just like I do now.

Even though I presently live in Louisville, Kentucky, it's always nice to go back home to Williamsport where I grew up in the shadow of Little League Baseball. On Monday, August 26th, the day after Valley Sports won the 2002 Little League World Series Title, the team from Valley Sports was doing exactly the opposite. They were getting ready to leave the birthplace of Little League in Williamsport and return home to Louisville.

On Sunday night, their last evening spent in Williamsport how had this championship team slept? As they jumped in bed for the last time in International Grove, were they still keyed up as world champions or did they just simply collapse, the long climb to Williamsport finally over–now they could go back home.

The championship game may have well been over, but the unveiling of days of star status would begin the next morning when team members would appear on ABC's "Good Morning America," and NBC's "Today." Additional honors were stacked upon Aaron Alvey and Zack Osbourne since they were named members of the Williamsport Little League World Series All-Star Team. Osbourne was the year's best shortstop and Alvey shared top pitching accolades alongside Walker Kelly from Texas.

Later in the day when the team had been taken across the river to the airport for the flight back to Louisville, I'm sure the coaches and the players, as well, were anxious to get back home as they carried with them the trophy of the Little League World Series. As their plane left Williamsport's small airport, which it is in comparison to Louisville International Airport, these twelve players would be returning to their everyday lives of going to school and spending time with friends back home.

The Little League Complex really isn't that far from the airport and I wonder if any of the players looked down upon the stadium where they became world champions? I wonder if Casey Jordan took a moment to think about the great catch he made to end the final game or if Aaron Alvey relived that mortal first inning home run that devastated the team from Japan? As the aircraft eventually disappeared up into the clouds, the Little League World Champions were already on cloud nine as they had accomplished what two months earlier seemed almost impossible.

At 7:20 p.m., their flight touched down in Louisville. Coach Troy Osbourne's comments that it was going to be an eye-opening experience when they got back home was right on the money. As airport fire trucks met the plane, and before the Valley Sports players could disembark, firemen used fire hoses to create a watered celebration arch over the plane.

LITTLE BIG MEN

There was an hour delay at the airport while the boys waited for their parents to arrive on buses coming in from Williamsport. During the short delay, the team was swarmed by fans desiring autographs on everything from baseballs to tee shirts. From the time the team stepped down from the plane, they were surrounded by the news media and public officials. It seemed like everyone, including baggage handlers, were wearing Valley Sports' tee shirts.

Following the entrance of parents, it was off to Cardinal Stadium where approximately 10,000 local fans eagerly awaited the arrival of the 2002 Little League World Champions. Supporters had been filing into the stadium since 6:00 p.m. and weathered a lengthy rain to greet the boys back home.

When the players stepped down from the trolley that had transported the team to the stadium, fans rose to their feet in cheerful applause as they chanted, "USA...USA." One by one, the players walked through the pouring rain to the pitcher's mound seemingly amazed by all the attention.

The master of ceremonies for the occasion asked Aaron Alvey this question, "You knew inside the whole time you were going to win this thing?" Aaron's response was simply, "Yes sir."

During the thirty-five-minute observation, the team was honored by a group of officials from the mayor of the city, who informed the team that signs would be erected at the entrances of the city in honor of their accomplishments, to a U.S. Representative who promised them that they would get to meet President Bush. The ecstatic occasion finally closed with the song, "We Are the Champions." Players shook hands and autographed everything they were handed. Television helicopters hovered over the stadium, beaming the ceremony live into homes throughout the city.

Comments from parents and fans alike were varied:

"I have never in my life experienced anything like this."
"When I saw the crowd, tingles went up my leg."
"I'm really proud of the team."
"It's a memory that will last a lifetime."

Later that evening, I'm sure not only the coaches and players, but the parents as well, were back at their homes sleeping soundly in their own beds. They were back home, but the demand for team appearances and activities would not allow them total peace just yet. There was an offer to appear on "The Tonight Show with Jay Leno," a trip to Disneyland later in the week, a visit to the Governor's Mansion for a picnic, and an appearance at the much-rivaled football matchup of the year in Kentucky between the University of Louisville and the University of Kentucky. Then, there was yet another appearance scheduled at Louisville Slugger Field where the Valley Sports team was to be honored just prior to the Louisville Bats Triple A baseball game.

The list of upcoming appearances and activities seemed constant, with Louisville and Jefferson County officials organizing a public tribute for the players, more than likely a parade or motorcade. The mayor of the city mentioned the possibility of the players being designated as Grand Marshalls for the Pegasus Parade during Derby Week and a day of honor at the Louisville Zoo was also being discussed. The Kentucky Lt. Governor said the team would be honored at the state capitol in Frankfort.

Following a week of kudos and celebration, the motorcade that had been discussed earlier came to fruition. Thousands of local residents lined Dixie Highway and assembled at Louisville Slugger Field to honor the team. The procession started exactly where it should have–where it had all begun at

LITTLE **BIG** MEN

Valley Sports' ball field. Each team member sat in a Corvette driven by members of the Falls City Corvette Club as the fanfare made its way up Greenwood Road, then down Dixie Highway, which was decorated with balloons and signs. I remember working that day and recall very few customers being in the store as the team passed by.

As the players arrived at Slugger Field, they were met by the mayor as the crowd of thousands broke out in song, singing, "Take Me Out to the Ballgame" and "Centerfield." The players were showered with gifts: a local Chevrolet dealership gave each player on the team a championship ring and Louisville's own Muhammad Ali sent awards of autographed boxing gloves for each player. Each player was also presented with a personalized Louisville Slugger baseball bat. The team then lined up in the infield and collectively threw ceremonial "first pitches" to start the game.

Finally, the greatest honor that could be imagined came true for the twelve players from Valley Sports. President George W. Bush was scheduled for a half day visit to Louisville. After Air Force One touched down at the Kentucky Air National Guard Base, agents took the team beneath the mammoth belly of the aircraft. Coach Dan Roach, told the boys, "This is the president. I expect your manners to be above reproach."

President Bush descended the steps and met with the Valley Sports players for nearly five minutes. Bush, a former Little Leaguer himself, casually talked with the team as he shook the boys' hands, telling them that he was proud of them and as champions they had a responsibility to act as role models for other children and the community. Bush posed briefly for photos before he was sped away in his limo and a motorcade of police vehicles. The visit ended with a fifty-minute tour of Air Force One.

GOING HOME

It's now late April in Louisville, Kentucky, and for the most part all of the ballyhoo of becoming Little League World Champions has dropped off substantially. You can still see an occasional sign or hear someone talking about the fabulous season Valley Sports had the previous year. I suppose that's the way of the world. What seemed so fantastic just a few months ago is replaced by more current events.

There is one spot in Louisville where the wonder of it all still lives–that being Valley Sports Little League Field. I dropped by the field recently to take in a game. There is no doubt that this is where the 2002 World Champions started their climb to stardom. There are eight banners designating the team as world champions. A small sign on the side of the press box and one on the back of the small building near the entrance to the main field state not only that Valley Sports is the 2002 Little League World Series Champions, but contains all the names of the coaches and players.

The actual playing field is clean and well-maintained. The outfield is circled by thirty-three, four-by-eight sponsor signs with a four-by-thirty-two-foot space of green fencing indicating dead center field. Surprisingly there were two more championship teams from Valley Sports in 2002. Down the right field line, there are two sections of fencing displaying two Girls Fastpitch Softball State Champions for 2002: Junior Girls, age thirteen to fourteen and the nine-to ten-year-olds.

One of the most inspiring things about this field is just to the left of center field. There is a large sign picturing an eagle over the backdrop of the American Flag with the message: *"9/11 Never Forget."* As I stated earlier in this chapter, no matter how compelling events may seem at the moment, eventually they can become overshadowed by current events and it really doesn't make any difference if what transpired was considered good or tragic.

LITTLE BIG MEN

The day of 9/11 was indeed tragic and something we may not talk about on a daily basis, but it's something we'll never completely forget. Valley Sports winning the 2002 Little League World Series was and still is without a doubt a wonderful event that happened not only to this team, but to the city as well. We, as local baseball fans, will never forget what Valley Sports accomplished in 2002.

During the days that followed the team's return to Louisville, the players and coaches had a lot to say about the Little League World Series and all of the memorable moments of their six-game sweep of the tournament. The players' favorite memories were varied:

Justin Elkins– "When Casey caught that line drive, it was just unbelievable. The crowd roared."

Jake Remines–"It was pretty loud. Everybody was yelling, "USA.""

Wes Waldon–"I'll always remember how loud it was. And just being there...all the home runs that we hit and the teams that we played."

Josh Robinson–"When Aaron hit that home run against Japan and when Oz and A hit back-to-back homers against Texas."

Zack Osbourne–"It had to be hitting back-to-back home runs with Aaron in the semifinal game. It was the eleventh inning and we needed a run."

Aaron Alvey–Aaron's favorite moment came after the team arrived back in Louisville at Cardinal Stadium as 10,000 local fans were present to meet the team. "Just coming down here and seeing everybody support the team."

GOING HOME

Shane Logsdon–Shane's most cherished moment was when he pitched the first three innings against North Carolina. "Just pitching in the Little League World Series Tournament. I pitched a good game. My knuckleball was really good that night."

Alex Hornback–"Just going there and winning and playing baseball on that field. I have always dreamed of that."

Ethan Henry–"Just having fun and chillin' with my boys."

Wes Jenkins–"Just winning the game."

Blaine Madden–"I'll get to go the to Little League World Series, take my kids up there and show them."

Casey Jordan–One of Casey's favorite moments was when he snagged that line drive to end the final game. He recalled thinking, "Do I have it? I had to be sure."

Assistant Coach Dan Roach commented, "I have to say seeing them charge the field. I just wanted to stand back and look at their faces. They had worked hard all year long and a moment like that one doesn't last long."

Head Coach Troy Osbourne said, "The biggest memory is that Valley Sports is the world champion and living the dream. But the biggest thing I'll remember is being able to live it with my son."

In twelve days, on May 10th, I'll be going back to Williamsport to visit my mother. Just like always I'll walk the two blocks down to Little League, go out to the practice fields, sit in the dugouts, stroll by the International Grove and visit the Carl Stotz monument.

At some point in the week, I'll make the short drive across the river to that old field where I grew up playing baseball. As always, I'll also visit the Original Little League Field, stand on third base, and for just a passing moment, I'll be a twelve-year-old once again, playing baseball in Williamsport. I pray to God that if I ever lose the ability to remember the days of my precious childhood, that the Good Lord will call me home for that could be the only thing better than reliving my youthful days growing up in Williamsport.

I suppose that is the reason for writing this book. Memories! What better way to relive the 2002 Valley Sports team and the road to Williamsport than to put it in print. Just maybe, one of the players, the coaches, some parents or just an ordinary fan will pick up this incredible story of winning the Little League World Series in the future and read about this amazing team.

If it were possible, I'd have a copy sent up to heaven for Brian Davis. But then again, I don't really think he needs to read about the wonderful events during this unbelievable season. He already knows–because he was there every step of the journey with Valley Sports. God bless the players, coaches and parents of Valley Sports. And, thanks to Carl Stotz and the great group of people at Little League Baseball that makes the "Road To Williamsport" possible for Little Leaguers across the world.

—LITTLE— BIG — MEN —

Final Thoughts

LITTLE BIG MEN

In summarizing the incredible journey that Valley Sports went on during their 23 game run at the Little League World Series title, I learned some interesting things, one of which is that you can't say enough about proper planning. Let's face it—you can't leap a twelve foot chasm by taking two six foot jumps!

The coaching staff of Valley Sports definitely had a plan from their first all-star team practice all the way through district, state, regional and eventually the Little League World Series tournaments. Their disciplined daily workouts of five to eight hours per day was based on great pitching and rock-solid defense which they felt would win them many games. The following chart displays without any doubt that the plan worked.

Kentucky District 2 Tournament
Valley Sports vs. St. Matthews National 12-0
Valley Sports vs. North Oldham 8-0
Valley Sports vs. Camp Taylor 17-0
Valley Sports vs. Beuchel 14-0
Valley Sports vs. Jeffersontown 2-1
Valley Sports vs. Jeffersontown 8-0

In winning the District 2 title the above statistics display very clearly that Valley Sports not only had great pitching but an amazing defense that did not allow other teams to score runs. In the six games that they played in, Valley Sports walked away with five shutouts, and the single game where they did allow any scoring—it was just one run. In their first six contests they had outscored their opponents 61-1, an average of a little over 10 runs per game, which also indicates that this was a team that could hit the ball.

FINAL THOUGHTS

Kentucky State Tournament

Valley Sports vs. Clay County 7-1

Valley Sports vs. Morehead 1-0

Valley Sports vs. Owensboro Southern 6-4

Valley Sports vs. Richmond National 11-0

Valley Sports vs. Owensboro Southern 3-0

Valley Sports remained undefeated through the state tournament but with a little less flair. After all, the heat had been turned up a notch as they faced the best teams in the state. The above stats show us that following their first victory against Clay County they hit a roadblock in Morehead barely winning by a score of 1-0. They had nearly been eliminated—a close call. Their very next game against Owensboro Southern was an extra inning game that they eventually won 6-4. This game turned out to be one of two games where there was more than one run scored against Valley Sports. The five games played by Valley Sports during the state tournament netted them three more shutouts. In the state playoffs they outscored their opponents by a margin of 28-5 with an average per game of just under six runs which indicates that Valley Sports was still hitting the ball, but not quite as well as they had performed in the districts. Their run scoring total against opposing teams at the end of their first eleven games was an astounding 89-6.

Great Lakes Regional Tournaments

Valley Sports vs. Ohio State Champion 5-0

Valley Sports vs. Illinois State Champion 2-1

Valley Sports vs. Wisconsin State Champion . . .4-1

Valley Sports vs. Michigan State Champion . . .3-1

Valley Sports vs. Ohio State Champion 2-1

Valley Sports vs. Indiana State Champion 8-1

LITTLE BIG MEN

Just as each game got more difficult during the state tournament, now Valley Sports was to be confronted by five other state champions. The road had gotten steeper but Valley Sports prevailed as their pitching and defense shut down six opponents, allowing only five runs scored against them. They had outscored their adversaries by a total of 24-5, averaging just over four runs per game. Their hitting had slowed down considerably since district play but their plan of great pitching and defense was still getting the job done. After completing seventeen games they had outscored the teams they had played by a wide margin of 113-11.

Little League World Series Tournament
Valley Sports vs. Aptos, California 4-1

Valley Sports vs. Harlem, New York 2-0

Valley Sports vs. Clemmons, North Carolina . .4-2

Valley Sports vs. Fort Worth, Texas 2-1

Valley Sports vs. Worchester, Massachusetts . . .4-0

Valley Sports vs. Sendai Higashi, Japan 1-0

With seventeen straight victories under their belt Valley Sports would now face the best in the world. The question was, would their initial plan hold up? During the series playoffs they were considered an underdog in five of six games played. The great pitching and solid defense plan held as they went undefeated to win the Little League World Series allowing just four runs scored during the tournament, outscoring opponents 17-4, averaging just under three runs per game with a final tally against opposing teams of 130-15. In their twenty-three victories they averaged just under six runs per game while allowing .7 runs scored against them, not even one run per game, more proof that their plan worked impeccably.

FINAL THOUGHTS

In closing, Valley Sports was the classic example of how hard work always pays off. It's rather comical how many people in the world claim that winning or being extremely good at something is a matter of luck, but I find it true that the harder we work the more luck we seem to have!

—LITTLE—
BIG
—MEN—

Index

INDEX

LITTLE BIG MEN

INDEX

LITTLE BIG MEN

LITTLE **BIG** MEN

LITTLE BIG MEN

INDEX